HEALTH FOOD COOKING
Using Herbs & Spices

£1-50

Contents

D1742017

2 **Using this book as a starting point**

2 **Index of recipes**

3 **Herbs and spices in the health food diet**

6 **An alphabetical list of herbs and spices**
Alfalfa; Allspice; Almond; Angelica; Anise; Arrowroot; Asafoetida; Balm; Basil; Bay; Borage; Burdock; Caraway; Cardamom; Carob; Cayenne; Celeriac; Chamomile; Chervil; Chickweed; Chicory; Chilli; Chives; Cicely; Cinnamon; Clove; Comfrey; Coriander; Cummin; Curry leaf; Dandelion; Dill; Elder; Eucalyptus; Fennel; Fenugreek; Flax; Garam masala; Garlic; Ginger; Ginseng; Heather; Hibiscus; Hop; Horseradish; Horsetail; Irish moss; Jasmine; Juniper; Lady's mantle; Lavender; Lemon balm; Lemon geranium; Liquorice; Lime blossom; Lovage; Mace; Marigold; Marjoram; Marshmallow; Mint; Mustard; Nasturtium; Nettle; Nutmeg; Oregano; Paprika; Parsley; Pepper; Sweet pepper; Pistachio; Poppy seed; Raspberry leaf; Rose; Rose-hips; Rosemary; Rue; Saffron; Sage; Salsify; Sesame; Sorrel; Star aniseed; Sunflower; Tamarind; Tarragon; Thyme; Turmeric; Verbena, lemon; Violet, sweet; Yarrow

38 **Buying and storing herbs and spices**

39 **Combining herbs and spices**
Salad herbs; Strong herbs; Bland herbs; Salad dressings; Herbal fruit salads; Flavouring cooked fruit; Herbs and spices in teas; White sauce; Tomato sauce; Brown sauce and gravy; Soups and stews; Rissoles and nut roasts; Omelettes, quiches and other egg dishes; Oven-baked savoury pies and crumbles; Casseroles; Individual vegetables; Cakes and biscuits; Loaves and rolls; Pickles and chutneys; Curries

48 **Conversion tables**

Using this book as a starting-point

This little book is more of a herbal than a recipe book, and a brief one at that. I have attempted to suggest how valuable — medicinally and nutritionally — herbs and spices can be, and to point out the cheapest and most effective ways of obtaining them and storing them. Readers already used to using wild herbs may be frustrated to find some well-known herbs missing, but I have confined myself to those which I have used myself, especially when commenting on their medical properties. I only began using herbal remedies on hearsay advice from friends, and when I found these effective I was encouraged to experiment further. You can be sure that if I say a particular herb is good for healing cuts or relieving bladder infections, then I have used it or seen it used effectively.

If you wish to gather plants from the wild, buy a good herb guide, preferably one with clear coloured photos — for example, you want to avoid both hemlock and fool's parsley, which are poisonous, when looking for cow parsley, angelica and sweet cicely which look so similar. And do read *Britain's Wild Larder* by Claire Loewenfeld and Philippa Back.

I included a few recipes for unusual herbs and spices, but there was no room for more. You will find many of the recipes I mention in my other books in this series. For specialized areas such as macrobiotic and Indian recipes, again I would like to think you will go hunting at source for more and more ideas.

Above all I think I have made it clear that my philosophy with herbs and spices is to get to know them and then blithely to do exactly what you want. If the dishes you cook are appetizing for you and for your family and friends, then your recipes are perfectly valid.

I hope you will enjoy herbs and spices as much as I do by following that rule of thumb.

Index of recipes

Baked red cabbage	16
Curries	46
Elderflower squash	16
Gomasio	34
Lavender and apple sauce	20
Lemon achar	44
Mint jelly	24
Mint milkshake	25
Mint raita	24
Mixed vegetable achar	45
Nettle soup	26
Orange fruit jelly	20
Pickled nasturtium seeds	26
Quick mint sauce	24
Rose-hip syrup	30
Rose milk	31
Saffron milk	31
Saffron sponge	32
Savoury saffron wedding rice	32
Sesame fruit balls	34
Shrikhand	31
Sorrel soup	34
Spicy mint sauce	24

Herbs and spices in the health food diet

The area of herbs and spices is unfamiliar ground to many people changing over to a health food diet, and there is much to be learned if these very valuable foods are to be effectively used. Since they have no bulk, most of us have tended to relegate them to the role of 'trimmings' and flavourings, very much an optional affair. Spices in particular, are regarded with suspicion by many people as 'strong' flavourings which will kill the natural flavour of foods.

In fact, herbs and spices have both had an honoured place in the diets of all traditional societies since pre-historic times. If we compare what the Greeks, Egyptians, Chinese and Indians have to say about the healing and health-giving properties of these plants, it is noticeable how these cultures, widely separated in time and space, agree as to the value of the various herbs and spices. And, of course, herbs and spices have always formed the basis of folk medicine. Even sick animals instinctively know how to dose themselves with medicinal plants to cure a variety of ailments. So herbs and spices can make a very positive contribution to our diet, providing a range of vitamins, minerals and antiseptic substances that will help to keep us healthy.

That is very encouraging, but our diet should not be some earnest regimen designed to dose us against a variety of ills. Food should be tasty and fun, and here again herbs and spices are tremendously useful. No two stews, curries, pilaus or cakes need ever taste the same if you constantly experiment with your own blends of freshly prepared herbs and spices. A rather bland grain dish can be brought to life by a herbal garnish or sauce. But in order to use herbs and spices effectively you must become familiar with their flavours and properties so that you can blend them in unconventional ways with confidence.

The herbs we eat are almost without exception suitable for cultivation in this country, although they are not all native plants. So if you have even a small garden or, at a pinch, a decent window-box, you can grow some of your favourite herbs and eat them fresh when in season. Fresh herbs have a wonderful aliveness which is slightly impaired when they are dried.

Wild herbs
Many other herbs can be gathered wild and eaten fresh if you have access to some open land. Herbs to gather from the wild, if you have the chance, include comfrey, chamomile, dandelion, ling (heather), wild thyme and sorrel. A word of caution, however. First, do not destroy plants, nor over-pick an area. Remember that birds, animals and other herb lovers want to share your territory. Just pick a few leaves, seeds or flowers as required from each plant, leaving every plant capable of reproducing itself for the next season. Also, if you are new to herb gathering, you need a well-illustrated herb manual so that you do not accidentally pick a toxic relative of the herb you want!

Herbs and spices in the health food diet

The season for fresh herbs is quite short, of course, and for the rest of the year you can manage very well with dried herbs. If you can grow or gather your own herbs at home and dry them then you will have the advantage of knowing exactly how old they are. Those sold in packets can be rather elderly and will have lost a lot of their flavour. You could get a very disappointing impression of an unfamiliar herb if the first batch you tried was stale.

Drying herbs
Drying herbs is a very easy matter. You may be collecting leaves, flowers, berries or seeds, but in every case you should pick specimens in perfect condition. When you bring them home (which should be as soon as possible so that they are not damaged), sort through and discard any damaged pieces, then wash gently in cold water and gently shake dry or, if very delicate, dry on a towel. Do not collect herbs from industrially-polluted ground as you cannot wash off pollution.

Once the herbs are both clean and dry, tie them (not too tightly) into small bunches. If too many are crammed tightly together they may form mould. If your plants will become very crumbly and brittle when dry take the extra precaution of tying the bunches inside clean brown-paper bags with plenty of space inside. Any pieces which then break off will not be lost. The ideal place to keep drying herbs is in a cool, dark room where air circulates reasonably. If possible, hang the herbs from the ceiling so that they are free of contact with any surface.

Now be patient and wait. The time required depends on the fleshiness of the plant (which is predictable) and the humidity of the air in which they are drying (which is not), so it is best to go by appearances rather than by rigidly prescribed times. A delicate herb such as thyme may be ready in 10 days or less while a very fleshy plant like comfrey could need 2 to 3 weeks. When they are ready the plants will have retained a healthy, though slightly faded colour (no brown or yellow or grey, as happens if they are exposed to light or too much heat) and they will be quite brittle. If you are impatient and store them too soon, the moisture retained will cause mould.

Once you are satisfied with the condition of your herbs, prepare a clean, airtight container, either tin or glass, label clearly, lay out a clean sheet of paper and sort and crumble the herbs onto this, discarding any coarse or damaged pieces; then store in a cool dark cupboard. Herbs correctly dried on this way will be potent right up to the next growing season when your cycle begins again.

You may not have the time or facilities to set up your own little herbal cottage industry like this. It is interesting, it is fun, and it saves money and disappointment, but if you cannot do it then you must consider the best way to buy and store herbs. There are numerous herbalists and health food and wholefood shops now so supply should not be a problem. The most expensive way to buy herbs is in small quantities, elegantly bottled or packaged — very pretty, but not cheap. Better to find a shop where you can buy them loose by the ounce. Buy small quantities, say 2oz at a time, and then store as for home-made herbs. Ask your supplier how fresh the herbs are and if he has no idea keep looking for a more conscientious source!

Spices

Spices are really no different from herbs. They are the seeds, roots, leaves, flowers, or even bark of plants, dried but processed in no other way. They, too, have tremendous medicinal properties, and they do not deserve their reputation for being overpowering. They can be, if badly used, but in fact, only 3 or 4 spices are pungent and even these have a clean, distinctive flavour if properly used. The rest are just pleasantly flavoursome and aromatic like herbs.

Spices are not, however, easily grown outside the greenhouse in this country, so they are generally imported. Freshness is therefore harder to guarantee. For this reason it is preferable, where possible, to buy whole spices rather than ground powders, and to crush the spices at home just before use. You can use a pestle and mortar, a spice mill or a blender, and the full flavour makes the little extra effort well worth while. Again, small expensive packages are not the most sensible way to buy. Asian grocers as well as herbalists and health food shops will stock loose spices, and since you are buying them whole you can safely store them longer, so larger quantities can be bought. (I buy my favourites, such as coriander and cummin, in very reasonably priced half-pound packs; this suits our family of 4 perfectly as we use that amount before they become stale.)

In this book you will find I have described herbs and spices together in a simple alphabetical arrangement: the list is not very long and in addition I have included a few miscellaneous items which cannot be strictly classified as either herbs or spices, but which are useful for flavouring food.

Uses and recipes for individual items are included under their alphabetical heading and there are some recipes for blends of herbs and spices at the end of the book.

An alphabet of herbs and spices

only), in very spicy cakes, or in sweet curries once it has been ground. It is not a spice I use a lot because I prefer the individual sweet spices it resembles.

Alfalfa (Lucerne)

This is a grass which is grown as a fodder crop and is also suitable for use as a lawn grass. Nutritionally, however, the seed, once sprouted, is an appetizing and easily used source of protein. Buy seeds which have not been chemically treated, sprout them, then use the sprouts (which are small and hair-like) in salads and sandwich spreads, raw.

To sprout the alfalfa seeds, soak them overnight in plenty of water, then wash and drain gently, using tepid or cold water. Leave enough water so that the sprouts are very wet but not lying in a pool of liquid. Put them in a sweet jar, laid on its side, and cover the neck with a muslin or light cloth secured with a rubber band (so air can circulate but dust is minimized); put it into a dark cupboard with a moderate temperature. Take out and wash and drain gently each morning and evening for 4 to 7 days until the sprouts are vigorous but before any sign of brown patches appear. (The time variation takes into account the fact that the seeds will grow more slowly in winter.)

Allspice

This is not as the name suggests, a spice blend, but a single seed which has the reputation for tasting like a mixture of all the sweet spices such as cloves, nutmeg and cinnamon. It is not very common in its whole form in this country except in pickling-spice mixtures. Uses for allspice are in pickles and chutneys (in whole form

Almond

This is not a nut, but the stone of a fruit. Almond is a delectable flavouring for cakes and icings, but it is also an extremely fine source of protein and the B vitamins so necessary for vegetarians. The best form to buy is the whole almond complete with the kernel. Blanch (by plunging in boiling water), take off the brown kernel and then use the creamy stone whole or ground to a powder. Once ground it is delicious in milk drinks and puddings. The whole almonds can decorate and flavour cakes, tarts and flans (sweet or savoury) and can be lightly fried and used to garnish any grain or vegetable dish. When using is as a savoury garnish you need not remove the kernel if you find it pleasant.

Angelica

Great care is needed when gathering from the wild this large, celery-like plant with its umbels of white flowers, since it resembles many of the members of the hemlock family. (Hemlock is the giant over 6 feet tall, angelica is around 3 feet, but other plants such as sweet cicely and fool's parsley are similar.) The sweet crisp stems make a good substitute for celery in summer salads. Normally they are candied and used to decorate and flavour cakes. I do not like bought candied angelica because of the white sugar content, but home-candied angelica can be made with honey or brown sugar.

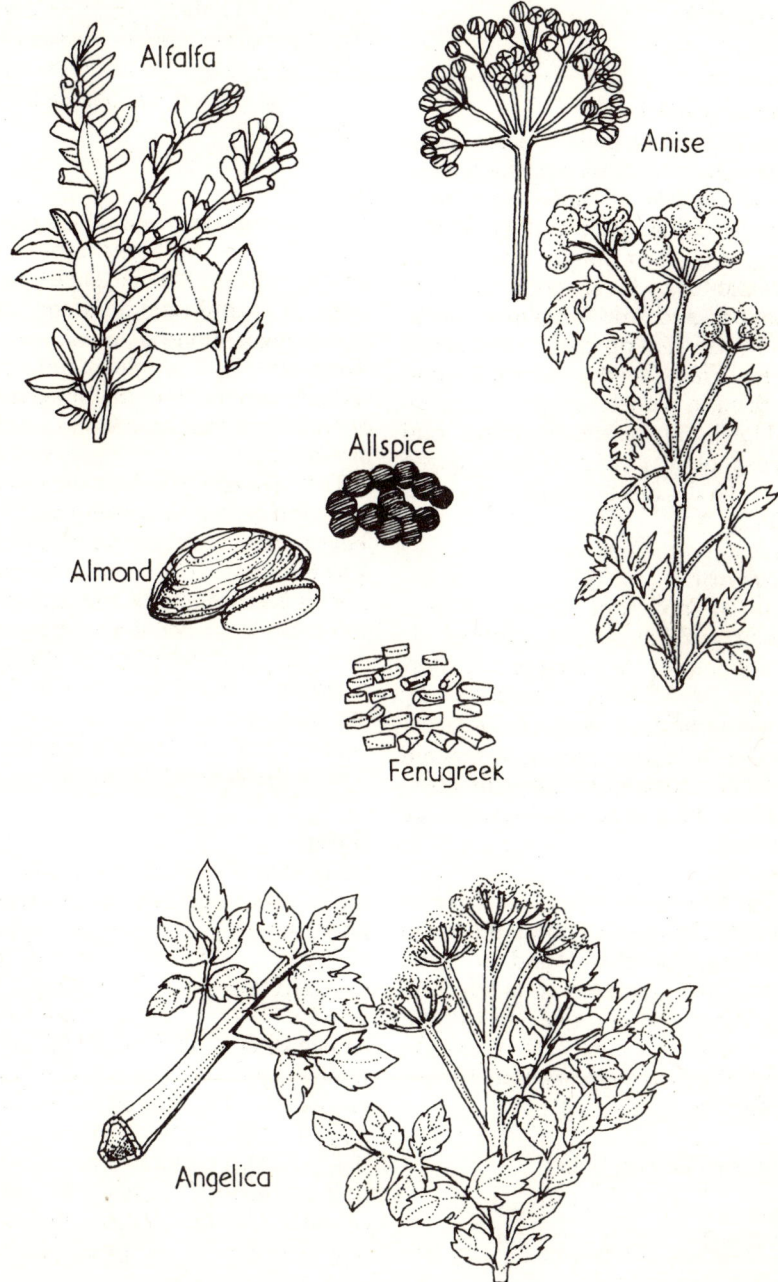

Alfalfa

Anise

Allspice

Almond

Fenugreek

Angelica

7

An alphabet of herbs and spices

Anise (Aniseed)

Anise is another umbelliferous plant of the hemlock family and the flavour will be familiar to every one from alcoholic drinks such as Pernod and ouzo, cough sweets and other confectionery. It is good for the digestion and for sweetening the breath after eating garlic. The small pointed khaki seeds can be ground and used in sweet curries (only very sparingly), in sweet chutneys and pickles, or to make a tea to aid digestion. (Just infuse crushed seeds.)

Arrowroot

Worth a mention, since it is a nourishing substitute for cornflour, as it contains more minerals. Unfortunately, it is being superseded by cornflour and is not easily available. But it can be used in all custard and sauce recipes in place of cornflour and being a starch it will reduce diarrhoea.

Asafoetida

This is a strong-smelling gum used in medicines but also found in some Indian curry recipes. It is hard to come by in this country and I find it too strong for use in vegetarian dishes. If you wish to experiment, use it sparingly.

Balm (see Lemon balm)

Basil

The leaves of a small bush, and one of the classic herbs of European cookery; it has a light, sweet aroma and flavour, – hence it is often called sweet basil. It can only be grown as an annual in this country so it is most often seen in its dried form which is suitable for use in stews and casseroles and in recipes calling for mixed herbs.

Bay

The large glossy dark-green pointed leaves of a small tree, the bay laurel which makes an excellent potted shrub if bought from a nursery; there is, however, quite a lot of wild bay laurel about. A single mature plant will yield a year's supply of leaves for drying without appearing heavily picked.

The leaves release their richly aromatic oil during cooking and 1 to 2 leaves are sufficient for a dish to feed 4 to 6 people. It is suitable for stews and casseroles, and it also appears in some curry recipes where it is called tej patta. Another use is in preparing custards – insert one bay leaf into the milk and soak for an hour, then heat the milk and discard the bay leaf before the custard thickens.

Borage

I only discovered borage 2 years ago and it has since become a favourite plant. A very decorative garden plant, it is squat with fleshy, slightly furry rounded leaves and startlingly blue flowers. When picked the leaves smell like cucumber. Both leaves and flowers can be eaten in salads, or the leaves can be cooked. *The Oxford English Dictionary* supplies the delightful information that its Arabic name means 'father of sweat' because it stimulates the sweat glands – this is a good thing in summer!

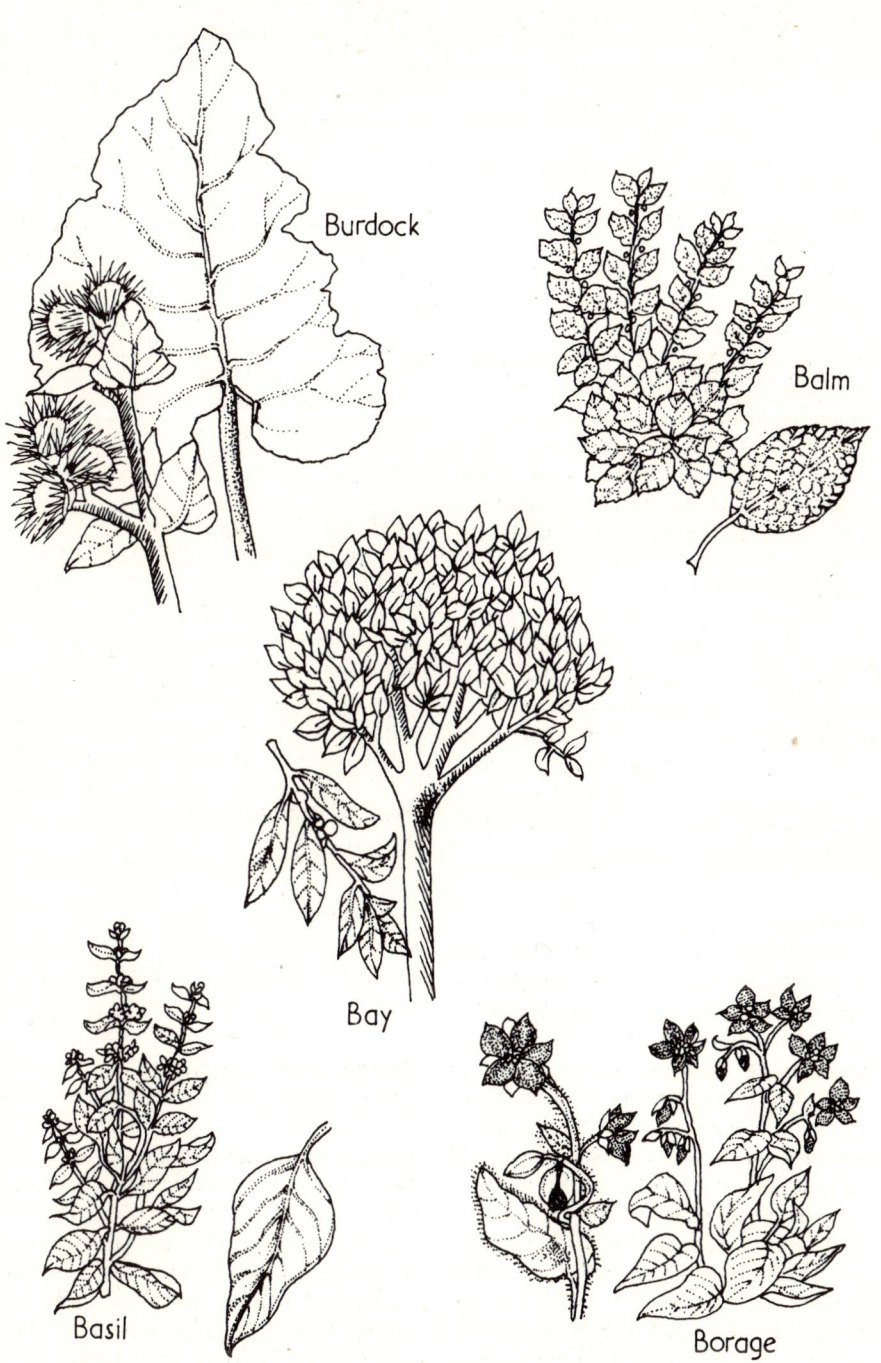

Burdock

Balm

Bay

Basil

Borage

9

An alphabet of herbs and spices

sweeter, and a wonderfully heady aroma; they are expensive but they go a long way. I especially like them to give both brown and white rice more 'zing'.

Burdock
Easily confused with dock because of its fleshy leaves, but not when in flower because it produces a liberal crop of burrs. All parts of the plant have been used in folk medicine but the most common form is roasted burdock root in grain coffee, said to help the bladder and kidneys and to purify the blood. The stems can be peeled and chopped and then steamed, sautéed, put into stews or even used as a salad vegetable.

Caraway
A biennial plant which, when grown from autumn seed, will produce seed in the following summer. The dried seeds are chocolate-brown and sickle-shaped, a little smaller than aniseed. It has a lively aroma and gives a nutty flavour to bread, biscuits and cakes. I also use it lightly bruised in sweet curries.

Cardamom (Cardamon)
There are two forms of this spice, one small and white, the other larger and greenish. Both are the dried seed-pods of a plant and resemble orange pips. Once the pod is split the little black seeds tumble out. You can use the whole pods or else take out the seeds and grind them. The white form is best in sweets, being useful in all milk puddings, in rich fruit cakes and in sweet curries and chutneys. I am not too familiar with the green variety which is said to be more bitter. Cardamom seeds have a light, 'silvery' flavour like cloves but

Carob (Locust bean)
This is the large shiny brown dry bean-pod of a plant used in the Mediterranean and in South America as a source of natural sweetness. The pods can be eaten like dates but are drier, they are suitable for use in cakes, milk puddings and milk drinks in place of sugar or cocoa as chocolate flavouring.

Cayenne
The hottest form of chilli (chilli itself is medium and paprika is mild). Usually sold as a red powder, it is the dried and crushed seeds of a form of capsicum. (Those red, yellow or green pods come in many varieties.) Unless you like very hot flavours, substitute chilli powder. If you do use it for the first time, err on the side of caution in measuring and keep away from the eyes.

Celeriac
A form of celery which can be eaten cooked — boiled or fried, sliced or cubed — or raw (grated) in salad.

Chamomile (Camomile)
There are many variations of this plant but they all share a characteristic apple aroma from which, the *Oxford English Dictionary* tells us, comes the name earth apple, or *khamaimelon* in Greek. The flowers and a few dried leaves, are used to make a delicious herb tea which is amber in colour and very aromatic, but mild in flavour. The plant in the

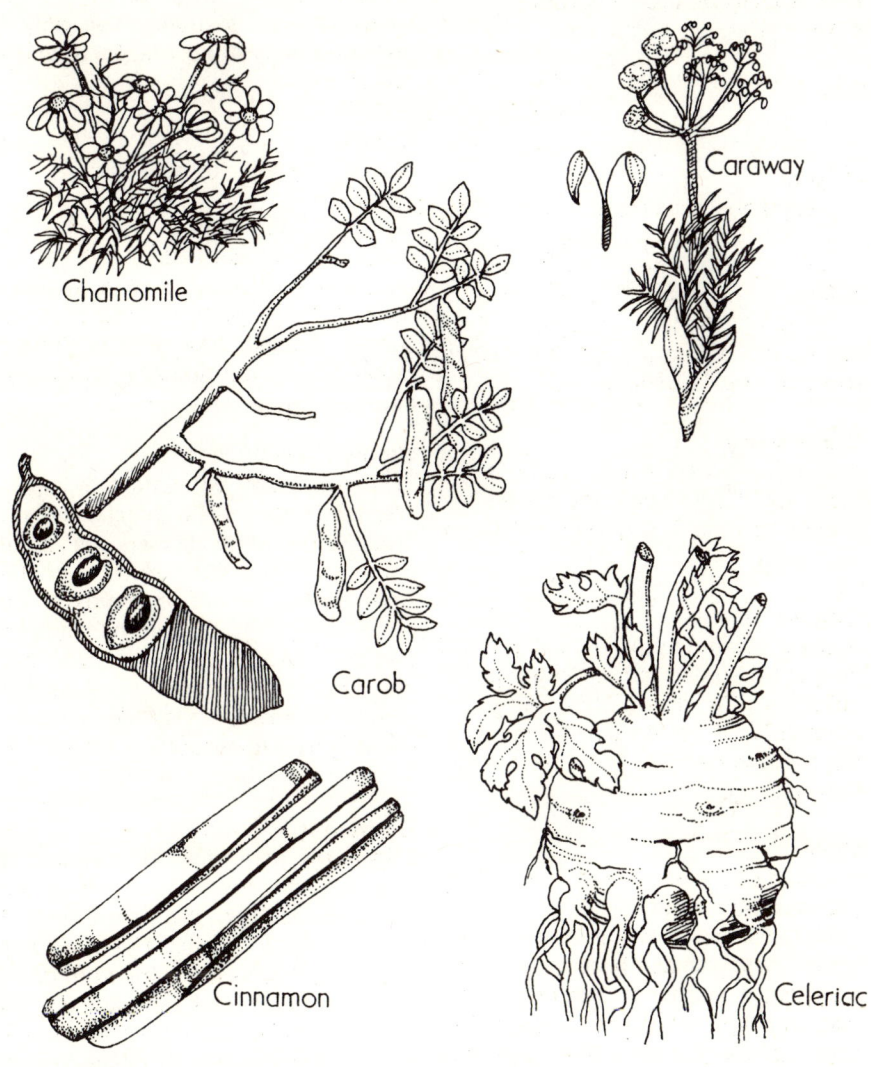

Chamomile

Caraway

Carob

Cinnamon

Celeriac

wild is easily recognisable, being a floppy furry plant with daisy-like flowers. Some say that only German chamomile will do, but chamomile I have found growing locally makes a perfect tea. The tea relieves mild stomach upsets and headaches and works very well in our family. Even the children come and ask for it when feeling unwell and they are both pre-school toddlers. The Elizabethans planted it as a lawn so that they could enjoy the aroma as their feet bruised the plants — a splendid idea. It also makes good shampoos and con-ditioners.

An alphabet of herbs and spices

Chervil
A prestigious cooking and salad herb in French cuisine, yet wild chervil is good old cow parsley and can be gathered and eaten fresh or dried in early spring. Watch out, though, that you do not mix it up with the smaller and toxic fool's parsley.

Chickweed
A common weed, a trailing plant with many small leaves and tiny white star-shaped flowers. It is good in salads or sautéed.

Chicory (Endive)
A salad vegetable resembling a small pale tightly-rolled lettuce and equally delicious, if slightly bitter. The root, roasted, is a coffee substitute. It is fun to grow because of its pretty blue flowers.

Chilli
You can buy this as a red powder, or you can buy dried red chilli pods or fresh chilli pods still in their green state. The small pods are very pungent, the larger and fatter ones so mild that if you like hot flavours you can eat them raw! When making curries or dishes such as chilli bean stew, I prefer to use one fresh pod finely minced because it has the sweet flavour of the capsicum family overlaid by the pungency. The fat pods, which can be bought from Asian grocers, can be fried in batter as a party treat, pickled, or even chopped into salted yoghurt or into a spicy salad. Do not over-use, as they drown the flavour of other ingredients. When first trying, use only 1 chilli pod or 1 tsp powder for a whole pot of food.

Chives
A small member of the onion family, easily grown and delicious in salads and cooked dishes through the summer. It is worth drying some for winter use as they have a sweeter flavour than onions and do perk up winter dishes. Like all the onion family, it is a good antiseptic for the digestive tract.

Cicely (Sweet cicely)
This large plant with sprays of leaves shaped rather like bracken, and umbels of white flowers, is quite common on both sides of the Scottish border and deserves to be introduced to gardens in the south of England. Nibble a leaf and you will get the gentle but unmistakable flavour of aniseed. Use the leaves in stewing fruit to reduce the amount of artificial sweetener needed.

Cinnamon
This is the bark of an Asian plant. If you buy the rolls of bark they are called quills, and this is the form I prefer to use in curries. The powder is best for cakes as it is difficult to grind the bark finely, but the bark will do well for milk puddings and milk drinks. I also use it in pilaus and in some chutneys and pickles.

Clove
The dried flower of a tropical plant with a powerful aroma and sweet flavour which can be bought whole or ground. Excellent in pilaus, sweet curries, fruit pies and stewed-fruit dishes. Soothes toothache if you can not get to your dentist quickly.

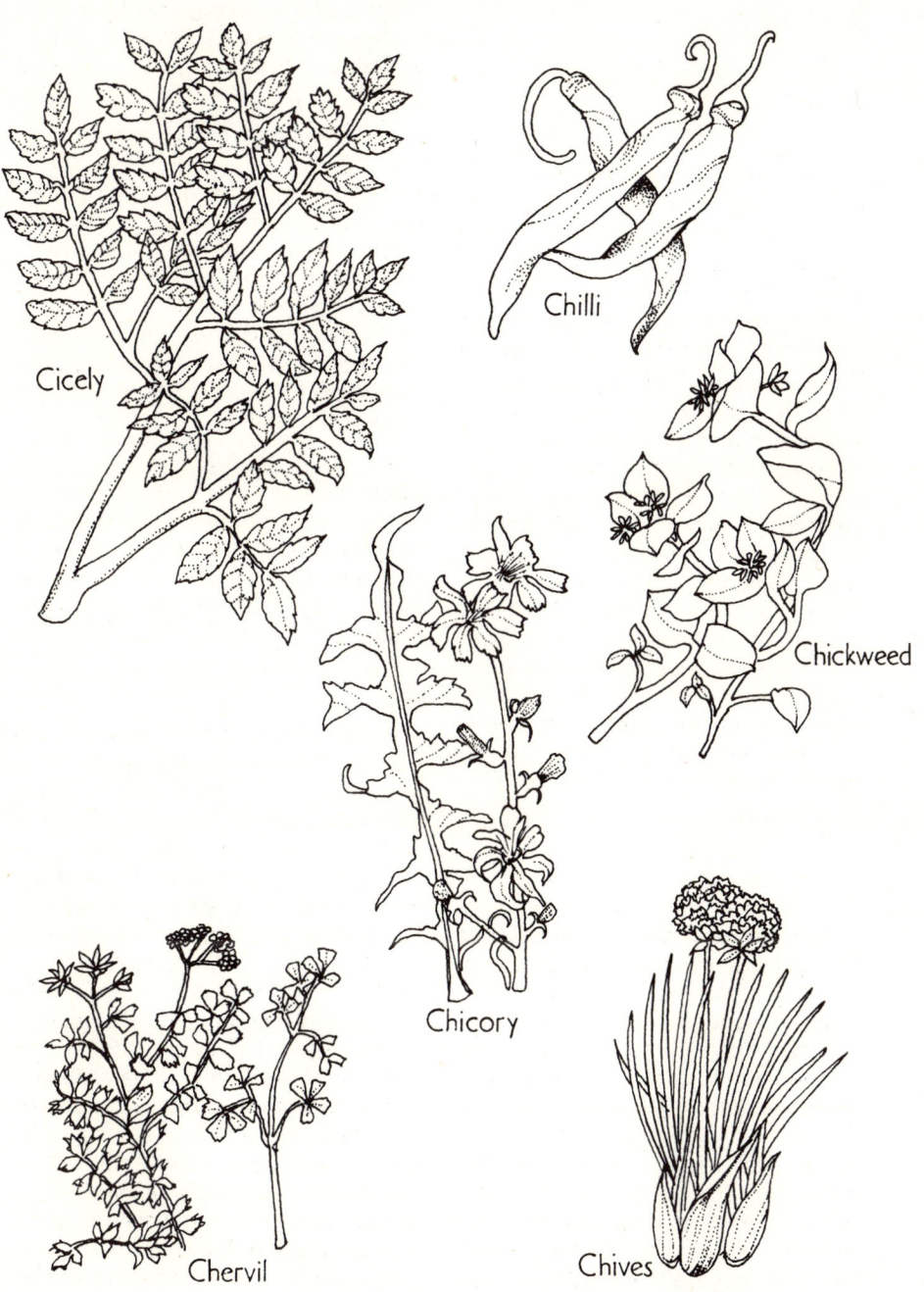

Cicely

Chilli

Chickweed

Chicory

Chervil

Chives

13

An alphabet of herbs and spices

Comfrey

A large fleshy plant which grows up to 5 feet high with big leaves shaped like spearheads and pink or purple flowers. It grows very well beside water. The large leaves can be cooked, the smaller leaves can be cooked in batter, dried for tea, or eaten in salads. This is a 'wonder' herb. A poultice of crushed leaves will heal cuts and bruises and sores rapidly, cold comfrey tea will heal even severe eye infections and comfrey ointment is good for all wounds. It is rich in vitamin B12. It was suspected of being carcinogenous when fed to cattle in concentrated form, but careful tests showed that the poor beasts had been given massive overdoses, about 200 times more than even an enthusiastic human would eat. It is now restored to its honoured place in the hierarchy of herbs.

Coriander

A wonderful plant which can be grown in greenhouses in this country. The greens, resembling great rangy bunches of parsley, are sold in Asian grocery shops throughout the country. Use them in soup, curry, mashed potato or salad or chopped in salted yoghurt. They have a mild flavour and pleasing aroma. The seeds, resembling white peppercorns, are among my favourite mild spices. When ground they release a veritable perfume while the pleasant flavour counteracts some of the more pungent spices in curries. I also use it with sautéed vegetables, in pickles and in salad dressings. All the ancient cultures of the world have valued it as a medicinal plant and particularly as a digestive.

Cummin

Similar in appearance to fennel and aniseed, cummin seeds are less overpowering and also less sweet than the former. Delicious with salads, especially tomatoes, with yoghurt, in all curries and in pickles and another good seed to chew at the end of meals to clear the breath. An excellent digestive.

Curry leaf

Not at all common in this country, this leaf looks like a bay leaf but has a more pungent flavour. You may come across it in South Indian dishes.

Dandelion

A most useful plant for cleansing the bladder, hence its common name 'piss the bed'! The leaves, flowers and roots can all be used. Pick the smaller leaves in either spring or autumn (they are bitter in summer when coarse), wash well and use either as a salad green, where their slightly bitter taste gives a lift, or gently steam or sauté. The flowers make a wine, and the roots of mature plants can be dug up in autumn when they are fattest and either sautéed like a parsnip or carrot, or cleaned, chopped finely, dry-roasted and ground to make dandelion coffee. The home-made coffee is hard work, so you must be an enthusiast to make it often, but the flavour to my mind is far superior to anything I have ever bought.

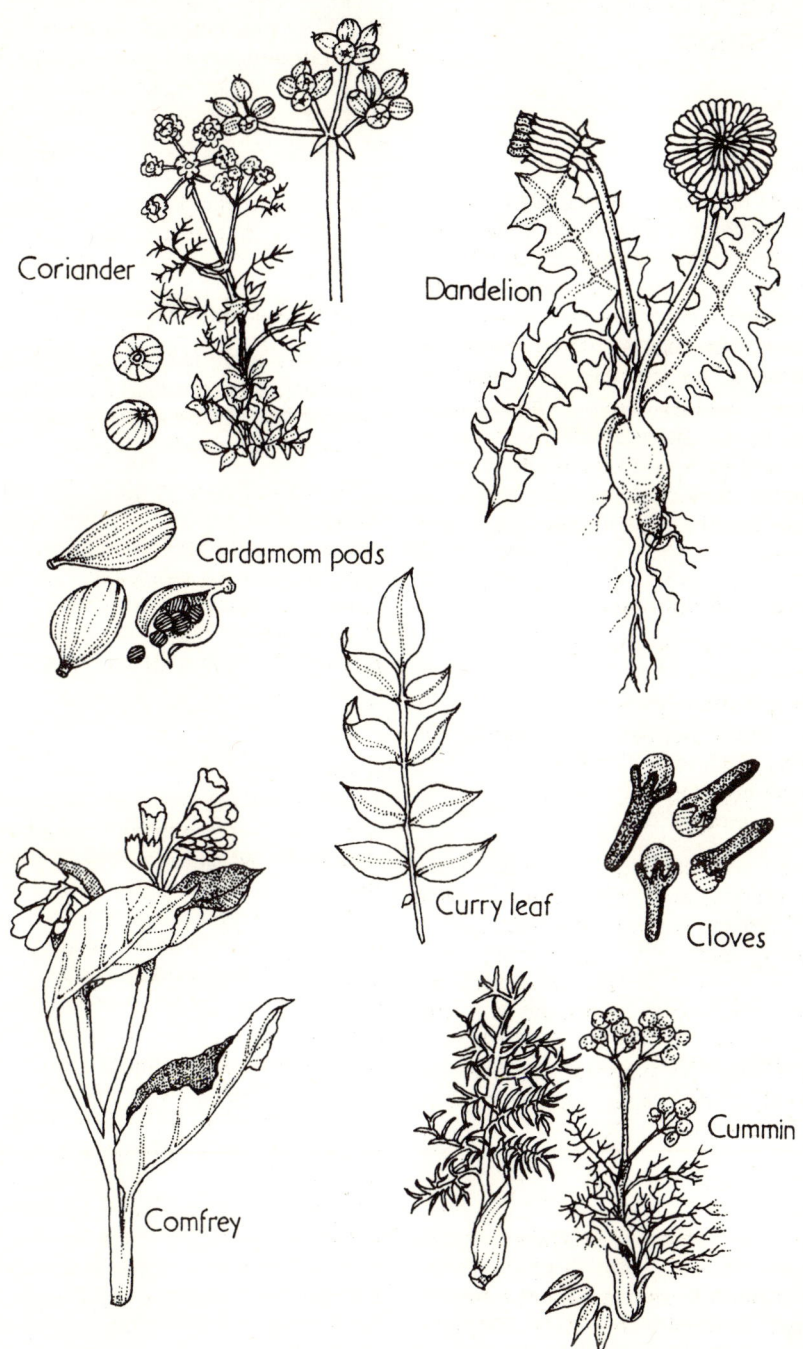

Coriander

Dandelion

Cardamom pods

Curry leaf

Cloves

Comfrey

Cummin

An alphabet of herbs and spices

Dill

Small, teardrop-shaped brown-green seeds which have many uses. An excellent remedy against wind and indigestion – dill water is the infallible 'gripe water' used for babies. I use dill in many pickles and chutneys: try making your own dill cucumbers (gherkins). I also like it for cooking all members of the brassica family and it is pleasant in yoghurt sauces, in lemon dressing, and in oven-baked red cabbage.

Baked red cabbage

1 small head red cabbage
1 large onion
3 large cooking apples
salt, black pepper and crushed dill seeds to taste
a little cooking oil
a little water

Shred the cabbage, coarsely chop the onions, and peel, core and slice the apples. Arrange these in layers, dusting with the seasonings, in a casserole or oven dish, pour over oil and water, cover and bake in a pre-heated oven at 180°C (350°F) Mark 4 for around 20 minutes. (If you have no dill in the house, clove is a good substitute here.)

Elder

Both the berries and flowers of this small tree are useful in many ways. The elderflowers can either be fried in batter, or combined with lemon juice, sugar and water to make a summer squash much loved by children, or dried to make elderflower tea. The elderberries can either be made into elderberry wine, or cooked sparingly with apples, or else combined with apples they can be strained to make elderberry and apple jelly. Both give a tangy citrus flavour to all dishes in which they are used.

Elderflower squash

1lb honey or sugar
1 gallon warm water
juice of two lemons
6 healthy elderflower heads

Dissolve the sweetener in the warm water in an enamel or non-metallic container, add the lemon juice and then the flower heads and leave to stand for 24 hours, then bottle and chill. A gallon may sound a lot, but this drink, tasting of lychees, never lasts long.

Eucalyptus

Dried eucalyptus leaves, resembling thin bay leaves, can be bought from herbalists; when bruised they release the aroma familiar from so many decongestants. Infuse in tea and breath in the fumes to relieve sinus trouble, or buy pure eucalyptus oil. Winter teas of mixed herbs can include one shredded eucalyptus leaf per jar to help against colds and sinusitus. The tea will smell strongly of eucalyptus in the jar, but when brewed the other herbs will not be dominated.

Healthy koala bears are created on a diet solely of eucalyptus leaves! So, although the leaves are only suitable for tea and inhalation for humans, they must contain many nutrients in their oils.

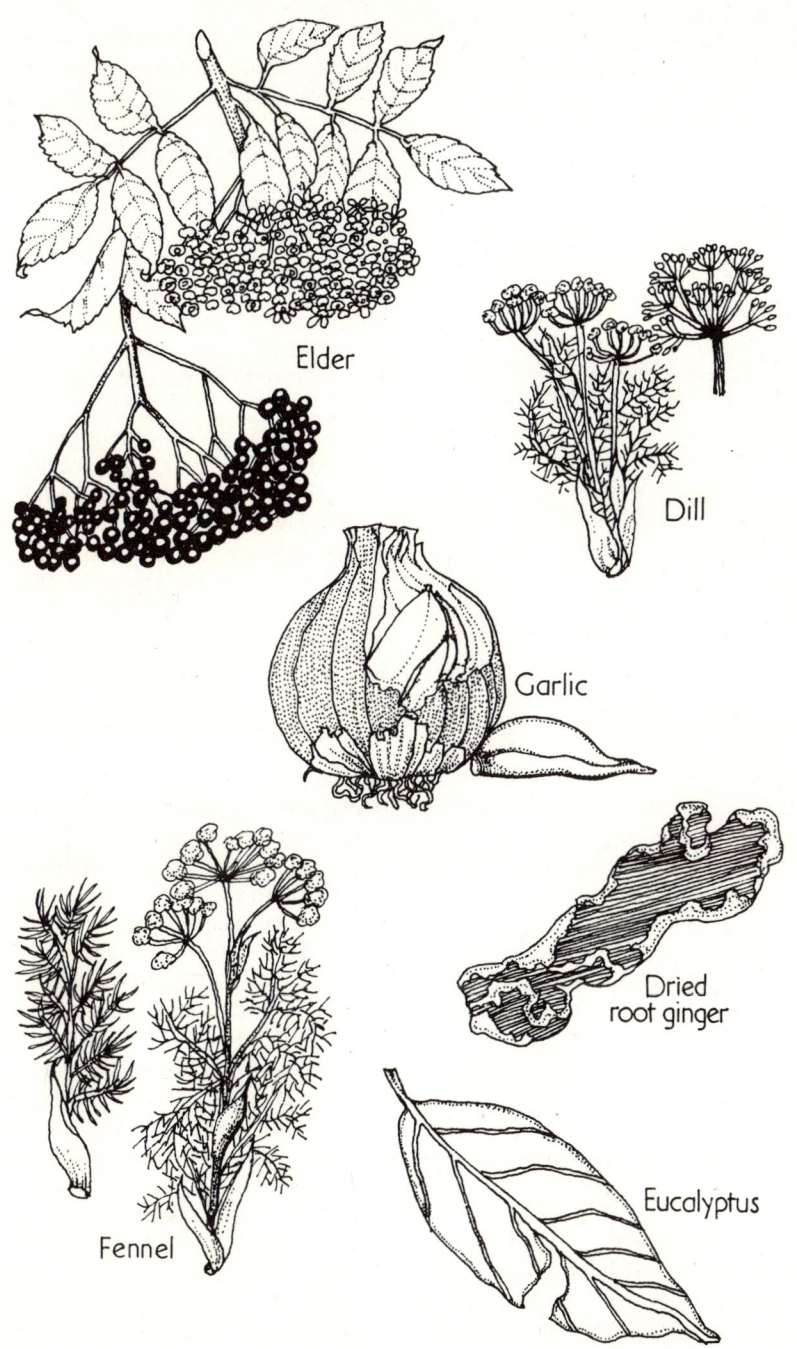

Elder

Dill

Garlic

Dried
root ginger

Fennel

Eucalyptus

An alphabet of herbs and spices

Fennel
As it is expensive to buy, fennel is an excellent plant to grow in your garden or allotment, but it is also very common as a wild plant in England, especially near water. The fleshy base of the stem resembles aniseed-flavoured celery and can be eaten in small amounts in mixed salad, but I prefer it sautéed or steamed and served as a side vegetable. Above this fleshy stem the plant becomes quite tall and rangy, with feathery leaves, and it produces seeds resembling fat aniseed. There is not much to choose between the two for flavour.

Try a few fennel seeds sprinkled on grilled cheese on toast (an idea inspired by Leiden cheese from Holland), or make a white sauce which suits fish or eggs. Crushed seeds make a refreshing tea. It makes a very cool summer salad dressing if added to a basic French dressing and it can be used sparingly in light sweet curries, especially if these contain sweet vegetables such as carrot, swede or cauliflower.

Fenugreek
I confine this spice to egg or mixed vegetable curries. It is a small square caramel-coloured seed. Use it sparingly because it is the spice which gives commercial curries their characteristic aroma and flavour and if heavily used it drowns other flavours. It is said to be a useful preservative.

Flax (linseed)
These small shiny brown teardrop-shaped seeds are available from herbalists and Asian grocers and are a herbal remedy for constipation. Ask advice from the herbalist.

Garam masala
This means literally 'hot spice' which is odd, since it is the mild spices which are used in this spice blend. I have stopped buying ready-made garam masala because I like to be sure of the freshness of the ingredients. My favourite blend is equal parts of cummin, coriander and nutmeg, with a generous pinch each of clove and cardamom. Other possible ingredients are allspice and black pepper. Garama masala is sprinkled on at the end of cooking, and I find it especially good for dry curries which have very little gravy. It is also useful in spicy fruit cakes, and can occasionally be used in either French or yoghurt salad dressings.

Garlic
If you are frightened of garlic breath, then take the plunge and chew aromatic seeds such as fennel, aniseed, or cummin after meals, for garlic has so many medicinal properties that it should be a part of the diet.

Taken regularly, garlic keeps the intestinal tract clear of infection as it is an internal antiseptic. The fumes of crushed garlic will clear runny colds and attacks of sinusitus. Garlic juice applied externally for half an hour, then washed away with warm water, will clear even persistent thrush. It sounds alarming, and it does sting for a few minutes, but there are no after-effects except an absence of the infection.

Use garlic in curries, casseroles, stews and salad dressings.

Ginger

This sweet but powerful spice comes in four forms: as a powder, in syrup, as a fresh root and as a dried root. I do not use the preserved ginger, even though it is delicious, because of the sugar syrup. Powdered ginger, if fresh, is best for cakes because it can be blended evenly through the whole cake. For curries, Chinese fried vegetables and other savoury recipes I prefer to use the fresh root. Just peel it and chop. The fresh smell and juices are much more exciting than the powder. I find the dried root, like little rocks which must be pulverized with a hammer, quite useless.

Do not use ginger with a heavy hand. It will drown other flavours and can irritate a sensitive mouth or stomach. Taken regularly it is another good preventive medicine against colds and sinusitus. Try grating a very small amount and tossing it through a large mixed salad. A pinch enlivens stewed fruits and makes them more warming in winter. Excellent in curries and cakes.

Ginseng

An inscrutable plant from the Far East. The best ginseng root is said to come from Korea and it is very expensive. It is best taken as tea, either alone or in a blend. It is a general tonic and very relaxing, but some supporters accord it a semi-mystical status.

Heather (Ling)

This is easily gathered from the wild if you live in the North. The tips and flowers of heather make an excellent herb tea.

Hibiscus

A dried tropical flower available (at some cost) from herbalists, which imparts a lovely red colour and pleasant flavour to mixed blossom teas. Since a little goes a long way it is worth buying in small amounts.

Hop

A hop pillow really will help you to sleep, so it is worth buying some dried hops from a home-brewing shop, combining them with other dried herbs and flowers you find pleasant, then sewing the lot into a cloth bag and inserting it into your pillow case.

Horseradish

This is a very common plant on waste ground, with large floppy shiny dock-like leaves and a plume of white flowers. You need a spade to dig up a section of the roots of a mature plant. Once at home, peel off the tough outer section to reveal the white flesh. This can be grated, seasoned to your taste and stirred into white sauce. We serve it with nutloaf and baked vegetables. The sauce will keep quite well in the fridge in a sterilized sealed jar.

Horsetail

You will only find this herb in specialist herbal shops, but it is worth tracking down as it is an excellent remedy for bladder troubles, especially cystitis. Treat the trouble early before too much damage is done. Drink one mug of strong horsetail tea 3 times a day and within 36 to 48 hours your symptoms should be clear. If a chronic condition does not respond, then you should have a thorough medical check. (It is not advisable to treat long-term recurring symptoms with home remedies unless you have a clear diagnosis — you could simply relieve symptoms of a serious illness.)

An alphabet of herbs and spices

Irish Moss (Carragheen)
Worth mentioning for vegetarians who may wish to make jellies for their children without the use of animal gelatine. Below is a recipe for mixed-fruit orange jelly.

Orange fruit jelly

1pt orange juice or ½pt water and ½pt orange juice
1 tbsp honey
1½ – 2 heaped tsp powdered Irish Moss or Agar-agar (Japanese moss)
2 tbsp chopped fresh fruit

Have your jelly dish ready. Heat the liquid but do not allow to boil and then dissolve in it first the honey and then the Irish moss; pour into the serving dish. Sprinkle in the chopped fruits then leave a few hours in a fridge or very cool place to set. When firm you can decorate with chopped nuts, coconut, more fruit or cream, or serve with ice cream.

Jasmine
Dried jasmine makes a bland-tasting tea with a superb scent. It is ideally suited for clearing the palate between the many different dishes in a traditional Chinese meal. A word of caution: although you brew jasmine like any other tea, it can become very bitter if left to stand. So if you do not want to drink it at once, strain out the leaves.

Juniper
About the size of a small green pea, juniper berries are a dark purple, almost black, fruit found on a common evergreen. If dried they can be used in any recipe calling for bay leaves, so they are useful in soups, stews, casseroles and curries. Friends also recommend them cooked in with boiled rice, and in salads, both fresh and dried. One berry is equivalent in potency to one bay leaf. The berries can be eaten of course, so need not be discarded after cooking. They are helpful in regulating bladder and kidneys.

Lavender
The flowers of lavender can be bought from herbalists or gathered and dried from your own garden; then they are an excellent ingredient in mixed-flower herb teas. Used in small quantities, because of their very powerful aroma.

My children also enjoy lavender and apple sauce poured over ice cream or milk puddings or even spread on bread.

Lavender and apple sauce

1lb cooking apples, peeled, cored and chopped
2 heaped tsp dried or fresh lavender flowers
1 to 2 tbsp honey
a little water

Put all the ingredients in a thick-bottomed saucepan, cover tightly and cook gently till the apples are reduced to a smooth pulp (just over 5 minutes). Now push through a fine sieve so that most of the lavender flowers are discarded. (If a few remain they can be eaten.) Now serve hot or cold.

Will keep well in the fridge in a jar for several days.

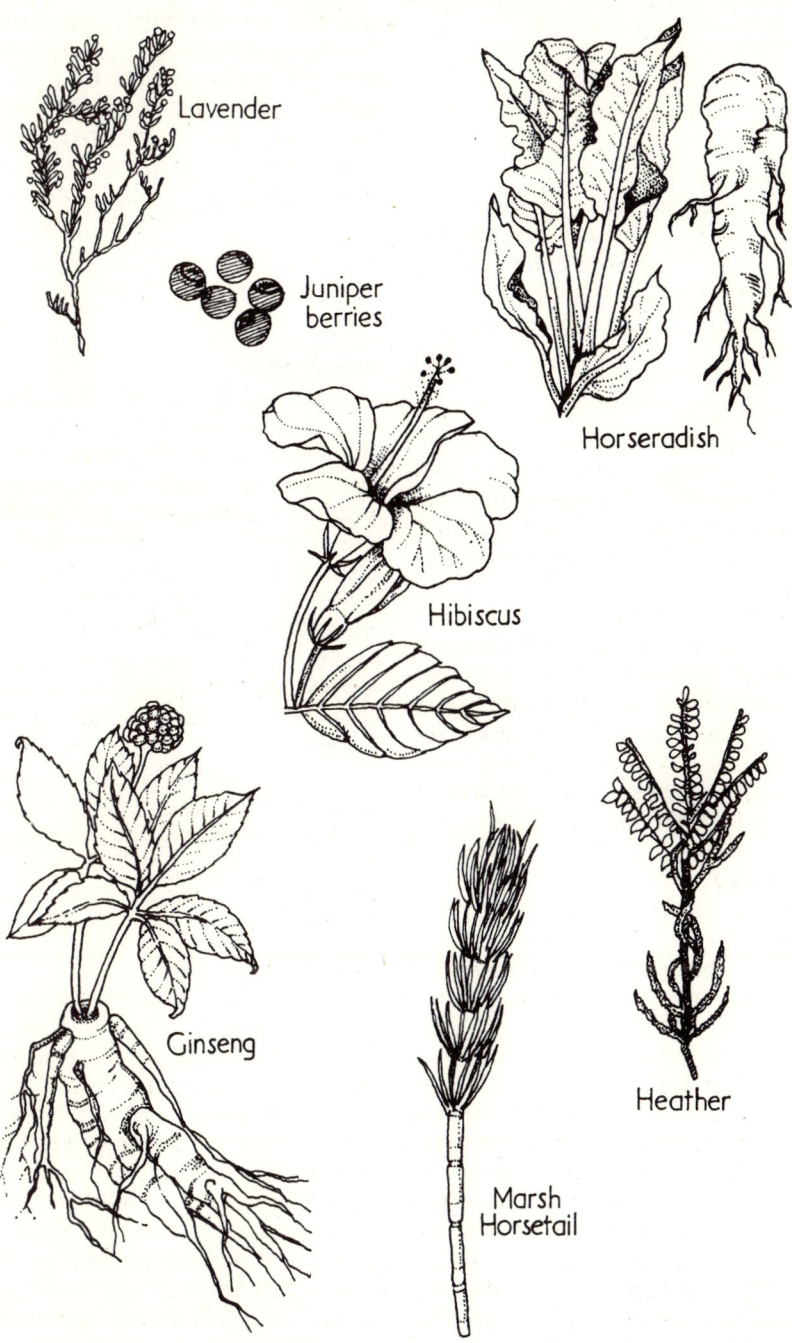

Lavender

Juniper berries

Horseradish

Hibiscus

Ginseng

Marsh Horsetail

Heather

An alphabet of herbs and spices

Lady's mantle
Can be bought from herbalists and perhaps from these health-food shops which stock a good range of herbs to make a medicinal tea for pregnancy and for menstrual difficulties.

Lemon balm
An easy herb to grow in the garden – fresh leaves can be used in salads. If you buy the dried leaves from your herbalist it makes a refreshing hot or cold tea. Both forms aid digestion.

Lemon geranium
This is the form of geranium with irregular leaves and almost no flowers (occasionally a few tiny white ones) which you see in Greek shops and restaurants. When rubbed, the leaves smell strongly of lemon. Use them in fruit jellies and milk puddings.

Liquorice
You can buy woody twigs of the liquorice plant for your children to chew (adults like them too), to stimulate the gums and to keep the teeth clean.

Lime blossom
A very pleasant herb tea which is said to have many medicinal properties. It is one of the best sleep-inducing teas, but probably it soothes inflammations and infections generally as it is also recommended by some of my friends for digestive troubles or for the relief of heavy colds, especially when these affect the kidneys.

Lovage
Another of the large celery-related plants. I have not found it growing in the wild but the dried form is very useful in cooking soups, stews and casseroles, as it is the herb found in most stock cubes. Fine savoury aroma and a good rich flavour too.

Mace
The outer part of nutmeg – mace is used in pickling and heavy fruit cakes.

Marigold
If you are growing marigold flowers in your garden you can sprinkle a few flower petals on to salads. (Nasturtium and rose are other flower petals you can use similarly.) The petals are quite edible and lend colour and aroma to the salad. The dried marigold petals are very useful for mixed-flower teas. Not only do they impart their pleasantly unsweet aroma, but they also give a rich golden colour to the teas. Marigold ointment is an excellent natural remedy for cuts, bruises and other small external wounds. Sometimes it is called calendula ointment, from the plant's official name. The flowers actually yield a dye, and can be used to colour rice or milk puddings.

Marjoram
If you are experimenting with growing herbs, bear in mind that there is an annual and also a perennial marjoram, the latter being known as pot marjoram. If you can obtain the fresh herb you can add small quantities to salads, and it is also a useful ingredient in summer mixed-herb teas. Once dried it is particularly good with oven-baked food so it is a useful ingredient of casseroles, lentil pies, nut loaves and all 'baked-bean' recipes (see also oregano).

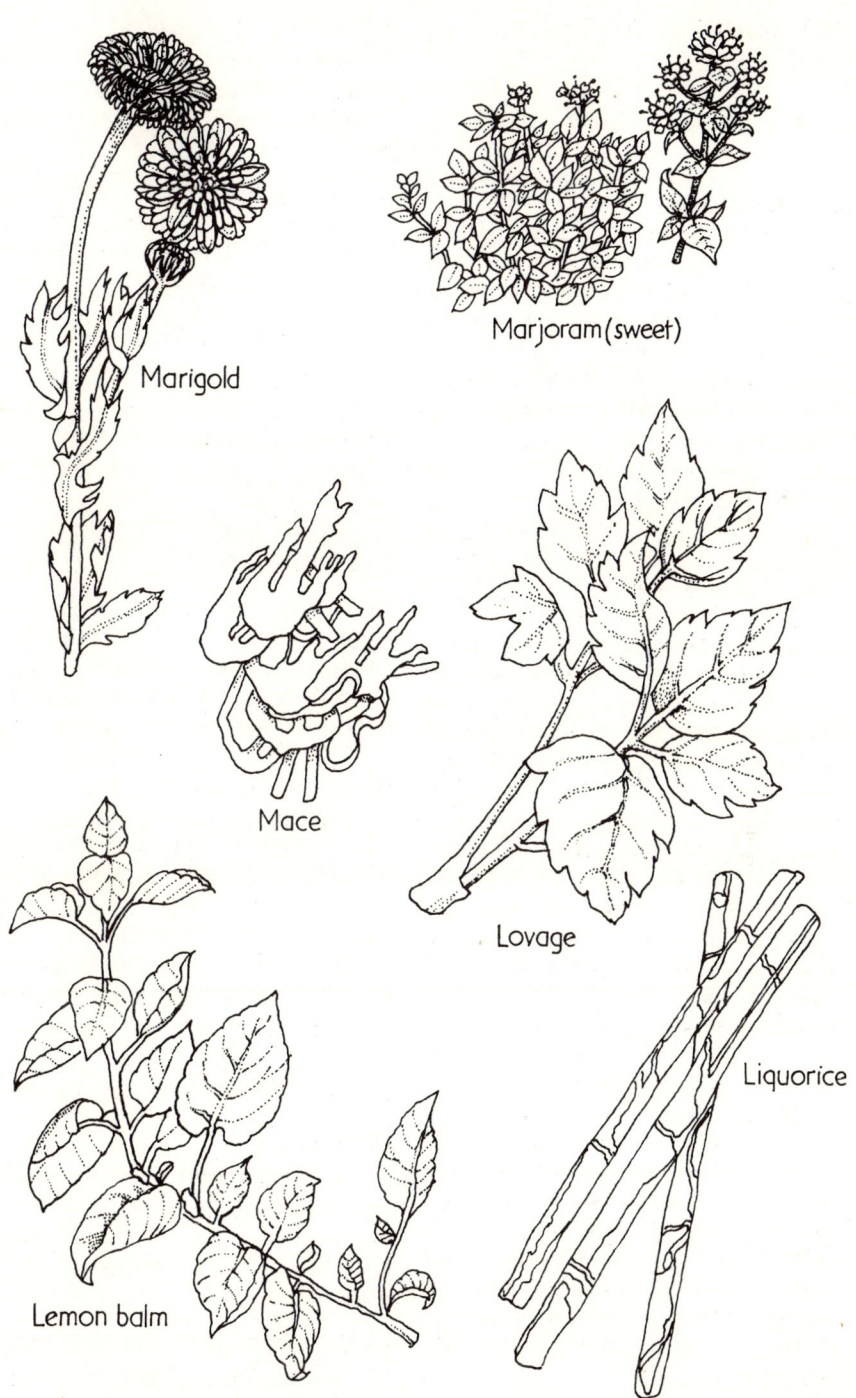

Marigold

Marjoram (*sweet*)

Mace

Lovage

Lemon balm

Liquorice

An alphabet of herbs and spices

Marshmallow

If you can gather this marsh plant wild, you can use the young leaves either in salad or as a cooked green. It is easily identified, with pink flowers and oval greyish leaves. However, if you do not live near a marsh you may find the dried root as a tea in your herbalists.

It is useful against bowel and bladder complaints.

Mint

You will come across many varieties of mint such as spearmint (the common one), peppermint, apple mint, lemon mint, eau-de-cologne mint and pennyroyal. A very easy perennial plant to grow in all its forms; in fact the creeping roots are hard to control! From the time when the young leaves appear in spring to the time when the flowers appear in late summer, you can crop the fresh leaves for a variety of uses. In summer I put a few raw leaves into salads or fruit salads and float them in fruit punches. You can also flavour salted yoghurt with mint as a delicious and refreshing side sauce to any meal. You can make mint sauce or mint jelly fresh: a world apart from the very standardized flavours of commercial mint products. A little can also be used in stewed-fruit recipes and in fruit jellies; you can make mint milk shakes for your children, and hot or cold mint tea for yourself. The tea is excellent against indigestion and stomach upsets generally.

Mint raita

1pt natural yoghurt
a little salt to taste
1 heaped tbsp mint leaves, finely minced

Beat all the ingredients together with a fork for a few minutes, then store overnight in the fridge. Next day serve as a side sauce. Good in mixed salad meals, with curries, but really pleasant with any savoury meal.

Quick mint sauce

1 cup mint leaves
1 dsp finely chopped onion
a little salt to taste
juice half a lemon
1 to 2 tsp honey

Mix all the ingredients and, if you have a blender, reduce them to a paste. If you do not own a blender, chop them as finely as possible then grind in a pestle and mortar.

Spicy mint sauce

To the above recipe you can add either half a green chilli, finely minced, or a half-inch piece of root ginger, also finely minced. Mint sauce need not be confined to meals of roast lamb — as a vegetarian I use it with oven-baked lentil or pulse dishes and with massive summer salads. You can probably think of many uses yourself.

Mint jelly

1 large bunch mint
2lb cooking apples
2pts water
1lb honey or brown sugar
juice of 1 lemon

Leave half the mint whole in sprigs. Chop the rest as finely as possible.

Have ready some small jam jars, sterilized and warmed. Peel, core and chop the apples and place with the water and whole mint sprigs in a jam pan and cook till soft. Now strain through a cloth, discard the mint sprigs and return to the pan. Add the honey or sugar, the chopped mint and lemon juice, bring to the boil and cook for 10 minutes. Now pour into warmed jars, seal, and store. Other herbs can be made into jellies using this basic recipe. Small jars of herb jellies make excellent gifts.

Mint milkshake

1 dsp honey
1pt milk
1 heaped tbsp chopped mint leaves

Stir the honey into the milk and, if you have a blender, reduce the mint leaves to a pulp. If not, chop them as finely as possible and grind in a pestle and mortar as smoothly as you can. Now beat the mint into the milk for 5 minutes with a rotary beater, then chill. When serving, beat up again, and strain if your leaves are coarse.

Mustard

There are two species of mustard plant, the white and the black, of which the black is the more pungent. The white mustard greens can be eaten as a salad with cress. The seeds of mustard are ground to the characteristic yellow powder which is so powerful. I prefer the Indian way of using the whole mustard seeds — they are like chocolate-brown pin-heads. They should be roasted in the frying pan to release their flavour before adding to curries — and watch out, they leap about like popcorn so keep a lid on! Indians also cook mustard greens like spinach.

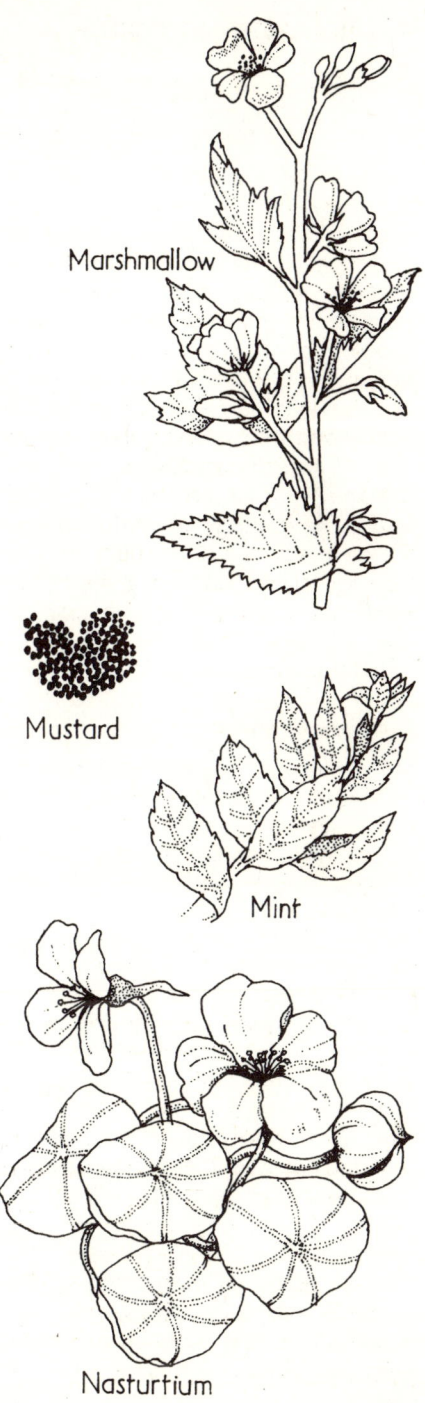

Marshmallow

Mustard

Mint

Nasturtium

An alphabet of herbs and spices

Nasturtium

This must be the most under-rated and most useful flower in the English garden. The round leaves of nasturtiums can be used as a salad green, but sparingly as they have a very peppery flavour. The petals of the flowers can also be added to salads and fruit salads or sprinkled on top of jellies, puddings and fruit punches — they are perfectly edible and come in many delightful colours. The seeds of the nasturtium can also be picked and eaten in salads; they resemble a wrinkled green pea and can be pickled to make a cheap substitute for pickled capers.

Pickled nasturtium seed

2lb nasturtium seeds, soaked in salt water for a week — change brine daily
½oz pickling spices of your choice
a generous pinch salt
2 onions, chopped
1½pts white vinegar (preferably wine or cider)

Drain salt water off the nasturtium seeds, place in a preserving pan with the spices, salt and onions, and pour over the vinegar, then bring to the boil. Now pour into warm sterilized jars and seal. Let them mature as long as possible before using.

Nettle

Nettles really do lose their stinging quality when cooked, so take courage and experiment: they are a nutritious food, containing iron, and so are a useful pregnancy food; they also contain vitamin C, so are useful as a preventive against colds. The time to eat fresh nettles is in the spring. Protect your hands and collect a good amount of nettle tips and the most tender leaves. When you get them home you should remove any damaged or coarse parts of the plant, wash well and then cook. You can use them as a side vegetable, either steamed or stewed in a little oil and water. Try them alone the first time and if you like the flavour you could later combine small amounts with other spring greens to give a varied texture and flavour to your side greens. You could make nettle soup.

Nettle soup

1lb tender young nettle leaves
a little vegetable oil
seasonings — a pinch each of pepper, coriander, thyme and marjoram
1pt water
tamari to taste
juice of half a lemon
1 dsp miso

This will make a thin, clear consommé. If you wish to thicken it slightly you should add 1 heaped dsp arrowroot or cornflour, dissolved in cold water, towards the end of cooking and stir till it thickens.
Clean and trim the nettle leaves. Heat the vegetable oil gently in the bottom of a soup pan, and add the nettles with their seasonings. Stir well, and gradually add a little water till they are just covered. Simmer for a few minutes till tender, then remove from the heat and blend to form a purée. Return to the saucepan and add to the rest of the water. Bring just to the

boil and cook for five minutes more, then lower the heat almost to nil and dissolve in the miso. Test the flavour and add as much tamari as you desire, and if you are thickening the soup, put in your arrowroot or cornflour now. Just before serving, squeeze in the lemon juice; serve with whole wheat toast.

You can dry the leaves you gather or buy nettle tea from a herbalist. It is a good tea to drink to prevent anaemia and it is a useful leaf herb to mix with dried flowers in mixed-blossom teas.

Nutmeg

A tropical import which is not easily grown in this country. Ready-pow-dered nutmeg is often stale so I prefer to buy whole nutmegs and grate off fresh slivers when I need to. An excellent sweet spice for use in milk puddings, milk drinks, fruit cakes and spicy cakes and sweet curries; I find it very well suited to savoury dishes featuring vegetables such as cauliflower, swede, parsnip and pumpkin. Useful, in fact, in most savoury white sauces. It can also be an ingredient of garam masala mixtures and mixed-spice teas. A stimulant of the digestion.

Oregano

This is, in fact, wild marjoram, a tougher, less sweet form of that delicious herb. If you are lucky enough to find it growing wild, or if you cultivate it at home, you can use the fresh leaves in small quantities in salads. The fresh or dried leaves are excellent in small quantities in all casseroles, vegetables or lentil pies, and in oven-baked dishes generally since baking seems to suit this herb more than stewing.

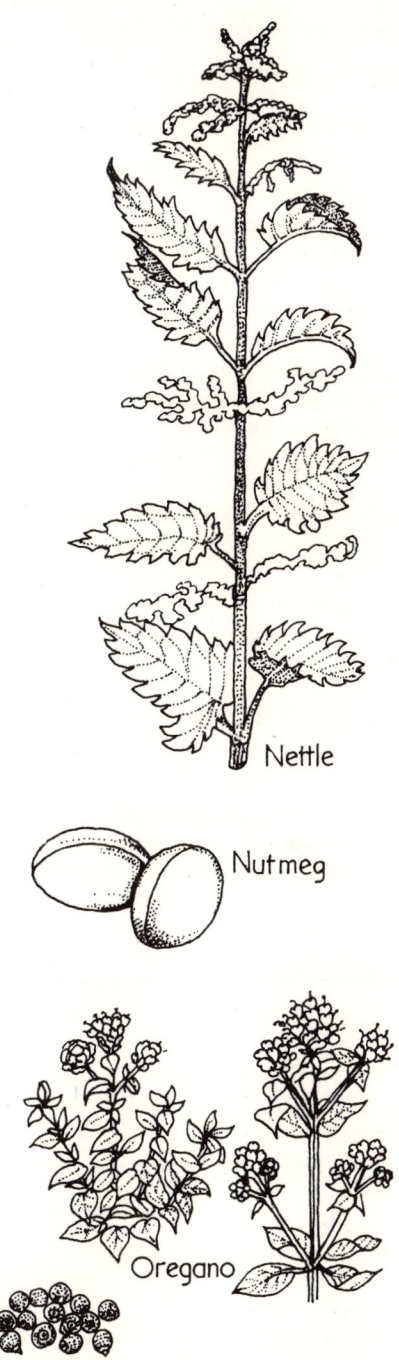

Nettle

Nutmeg

Oregano

An alphabet of herbs and spices

Paprika

A red powder made by grinding dried sweet red peppers which is an excellent spice with tomato-based sauces, especially in spaghetti dishes and bean casseroles. If you either dislike chilli or find it actually upsets your stomach you can substitute paprika in any spicy recipe to give a mild but flavoursome dish. The two spices are related, so you will get all the sweet qualities without the hotness.

Parsley

A very easy herb to grow and use fresh all through the summer, but I do not find dried parsley worth using as it loses its flavour so. Parsley is sadly underused, for it is rich in minerals and pleasantly tasty, yet so often it is used as a garnish and left untouched on the plate. Chop generous amounts of fresh parsley for inclusion in mixed salads, where it will give colour and texture. Sprinkle chopped parsley on top of any soup just before serving, and use it as a substitute for coriander greens in Indian recipes when these are not available. It can also be stirred into mashed potato or other mashed vegetables, and white parsley sauce will go well over bean pies, fish or eggs.

Pepper

Peppercorns are the dried berries of a tropical plant. The black ones have been picked before ripening, the white ones are ripe. Both forms of peppercorn are best bought whole and ground freshly in a mill before use. I prefer to use white peppercorns in white sauces and with all the sweet-flavoured vegetables such as carrot, cauliflower, swede, pumpkin and parsnip. For most other dishes I favour black pepper.

One unusual use for pepper is to include a little in spiced tea, an excellent Indian winter drink which is good for colds as it keeps the respiratory tract clear.

Sweet pepper

There are many pods of the capsicum family, which occur in many sizes and in every colour from green through yellow and orange to red. Have no fear of the large red or green sweet peppers, they have no hotness in them and are an excellent fresh or cooked vegetable. Dried red peppers of this kind form the light spice paprika. Smaller, more pungent members of the family can be bought fresh, or dried in powder form as chilli or the powerful cayenne – which add the heat to dishes like curry.

Pistachio

A nut prized throughout the Middle East and beyond into India. Though expensive it is an excellent sweet flavouring. You can buy salted or unsalted pistachio nuts in the kernel and they can be eaten plain as a savoury munch. However, if you remove the kernels and grind unsalted nuts they are most useful in making milk drinks, milk puddings or any of the Indian sweetmeats. They will not colour food the lurid green of pistachio ice cream, however – that comes from good old synthetic food colouring!

Parsley

Blue poppy seeds

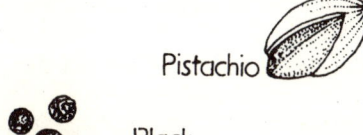

Pistachio

Black peppercorns

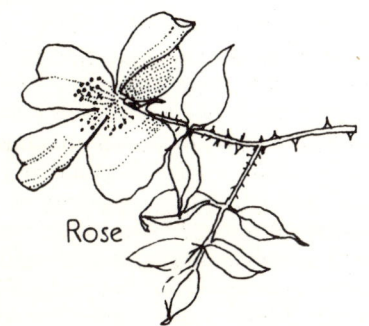

Rose

Poppy seed

These tiny pinhead seeds come in various colours and the cheapest way to buy them is loose from an Asian grocer. They are delicious on top of bread (glue them in place with a glaze of egg yolk) or in biscuits. I often include them with toppings of other seeds and nuts in savoury crumbles and other oven dishes. I have found powdered poppy seeds (called khus-khus) used as a flavouring for milk drinks in India where it was pleasantly unsweet.

Raspberry leaf

An excellent tea to drink throughout pregnancy and in post-natal care, because it helps to make the muscles supple and so aids in labour and in the later recovery of muscle tone in the womb wall. Try to drink it daily throughout pregnancy. If you do not like the flavour (I did not and I think this may be to do with first encountering it in conjunction with morning sickness), then combine it with one or more herb teas which do appeal.

Rose

Rose petals are used extensively throughout the East as an ingredient in many dishes. If you want to experiment, use the type of rose which has small thin petals, such as a briar rose or wild rose. Any colour is suitable but pink seems the most popular.

At Indian weddings the sweets and also the rice pilaus will be liberally sprinkled with rose petals and also with finely beaten, edible gold and silver leaf. You can pick a few fresh rose petals and sprinkle into salads or fruit salads or over rice dishes.

An alphabet of herbs and spices

In Iran (in the days when you could travel freely there) my favourite breakfast was fresh-baked unleavened bread, a great flap of it, with yoghurt and rose-petal jam. This jam is very sweet so I would advise you to buy a small jar (which will be very expensive) to see if you like it. If you are addicted then you can make your own rose petal jam in the summer. Rosewater, a distillation from rose petals (from, I believe, the damask rose) is available from chemists and is an excellent flavouring for milk drinks and puddings, sweet rice dishes and all oriental sweetmeats. Make sure from the chemist that it is pure rosewater and is, therefore, edible. Well-stocked Asian grocers also sell rosewater.

Rose milk

1pt milk
1 dsp honey
1 dsp rosewater

Warm the milk gently, dissolving in the honey until thoroughly blended; then cool to room temperature, put in the rosewater and whisk for 5 minutes. Now chill. Whisk again briefly just before you serve.

Rose-hips

Easily gathered from hedgerows in the late summer or early autumn (at least, where I live — perhaps later in other areas), rose-hips are the best source of vitamin C available, many times more potent than citrus fruits. Yet if you buy commercial rose-hip syrup you also get a heavy dose of white sugar and chemicals. So perhaps you would like to take the trouble to gather your own rose-hips and make rose-hip syrup at home. Once you have it, it makes a fine hot winter drink diluted with hot water, or a pleasant sauce to pour over puddings and sweets. It is always very popular with children and so nutritious.

Rose-hip syrup

If gathering rose-hips from the wild, look for the small dark red oval berry of the wild rose in the hedgerows. Do not overpick in your enthusiasm, for the birds need the rose-hips too and you will want the plant to remain healthy for next year. But to make all the effort worthwhile, try to collect about 4lbs of fruit. Arrange this for a day when you are sure you can make the syrup on the following day, otherwise the fruit will start to lose its valuable vitamin C before it is preserved.

You will need a preserving pan, a wooden spoon and a cheesecloth bag for straining the syrup and roughly 2lbs of honey or brown sugar. Have plenty of water available, and warm sterilized jars or bottles for storing the finished syrup.

When you get the rose-hips home, clean them, and top and tail, then put them through a mincer or chop them coarsely. Put them in the pan with enough boiling water to cover them generously, simmer for 5 minutes, then leave to stand till just warm. Strain through the cheesecloth and keep the juice aside. Return the pulp from the bag to the pot and again cover in boiling water and boil for 5 minutes, then cool and strain. Combine the two lots of juice and strain this once more. Now return the juice to the pan and stir in your sweetener. When thoroughly blended and dissolved, boil for 10 minutes and then put into your warm, sterilized bottles and seal.

Rosemary
One of the most powerful of herbs and really ideally suited to meats (especially lamb). I use it sparingly in many oven-baked vegetarian dishes such as bean pies, savoury crumbles and casseroles. A little dried or fresh rosemary can be included in any pot of mixed-herb teas and if you drink it regularly it helps to reduce mucus in colds and sinus infections. Rosemary jelly can be made, using the basic jelly recipe described under 'mint', and it makes an unusual and delicious accompaniment to pies and summer rice salads.

Rue
An evergreen shrub with yellow flowers which is easy to cultivate in the garden. Young leaves can be included in mixed salads in small quantities as both the flavour and aroma are heavy. Dried rue is sold by herbalists as a remedy for menstrual problems.

Saffron
The most expensive spice on earth: a yellow colouring with a beautifully heady aroma and a delicate sweet flavour. It is made from the dried stamens of a type of crocus. What a shame it is no longer a main crop round Saffron Walden! It is grown now in Spain, Egypt and Kashmir. You can imagine that it takes a lot of crocuses to produce a pound weight of saffron. You can either buy powdered saffron or the actual strands, the stamens. Either way, even a tiny amount is very expensive. It is, however, so delicious that as an occasional treat it really should not be neglected. Below are my favourite saffron recipes.

Saffron milk (Kesar dudh)

1pt milk
1 dsp honey
½ tsp saffron

Warm the milk and dissolve in first the honey and then the saffron. Cool to room temperature and chill overnight in the fridge. When needed the next day, whisk thoroughly for 5 minutes with a rotary beater before serving.

Shrikhand (Saffron yoghurt sweet)

2pts natural yoghurt
2 dsp honey
½ tsp each of ground nutmeg and cardamom
1 tsp saffron

You will need a cheesecloth bag (a white pillowcase would do) to drip the yoghurt. Put the yoghurt into the cloth bag and hang it in a cool place with a bowl beneath to catch the whey. Leave it until it stops dripping, which may be 45 minutes to 3 hours, depending on the texture of your yoghurt.

Once the yoghurt in the bag is very thick, carefully stir in the honey (which could be warmed first to help it dissolve) and the spices. Beat well, then chill overnight in the fridge. Stir before serving.

This yoghurt should be eaten in small quantities as it is very rich. The Indian version is very sweet, containing a lot of castor sugar.

An alphabet of herbs and spices

Savoury saffron wedding rice

1lb long-grain brown rice
water for cooking
1oz saffron
salt to taste
1 flat tsp each of the following seasonings:
    black peppercorns
    cinnamon bark
    juniper berries
    cloves
    cardamom

Leave the juniper berries whole. Take all the spices in their whole form and crush coarsely.

Place the washed rice in a heavy saucepan with 1½ times its volume of cold water and stir in all the seasonings. Bring up to the boil, and immediately lower the heat so that the rice can simmer steadily. When it comes to the boil, skim off any dark scum but not normal white froth. Now put on the lid and simmer for 40 minutes without uncovering or stirring. Now check whether it is tender and allow to continue on a low heat with the lid off until it absorbs all its water.

Traditionally this would be eaten with curries but it is so very delicious that I also like to serve it with lighter-flavoured foods so that it can be appreciated for its own sake: try it with a more bland casserole, with vegetable kebabs or even with salads. An equally colourful but less subtly-flavoured cheaper dish can be made by substituting turmeric for saffron in the above recipe.

Saffron sponge

1 tbsp milk
1 tsp saffron
4 eggs
4oz pure honey
4oz of 85 per cent flour
a pinch salt

Warm the milk and dissolve the saffron in it and then leave to stand. Separate the eggs and beat the yolks. Add the saffron milk and the honey and beat well. (In cold weather warm the honey first.) Slowly add the flour after sieving it with the salt. Beat gently but quickly. Whisk the egg whites and fold these in too to produce a relatively liquid batter. Pour into two oiled 8 inch diameter baking tins and cook in a pre-heated oven at 170°C (325°F) Mark 3, for 25 minutes. Turn out and cool on a wire rack. Decorate if you wish with whipped cream but basically keep the cake plain so you can enjoy its flavour.

Sage
Another quite heavily-flavoured oily herb. For this reason it is ideal with meat and poultry. In non-meat cooking I personally like sage in rissoles and with oven-baked vegetables or pulses. Either fresh or dried it is a useful ingredient of mixed-herb teas, used in small quantities. If you take it at least 3 times a week from early autumn on, it is one of the best teas against sinus trouble. It is an old Greek remedy against colds and was given to me by a Greek friend who had been regularly dosed with it as a child.

Salsify
Even if you do find wild salsify it would not be advisable to pick it, for

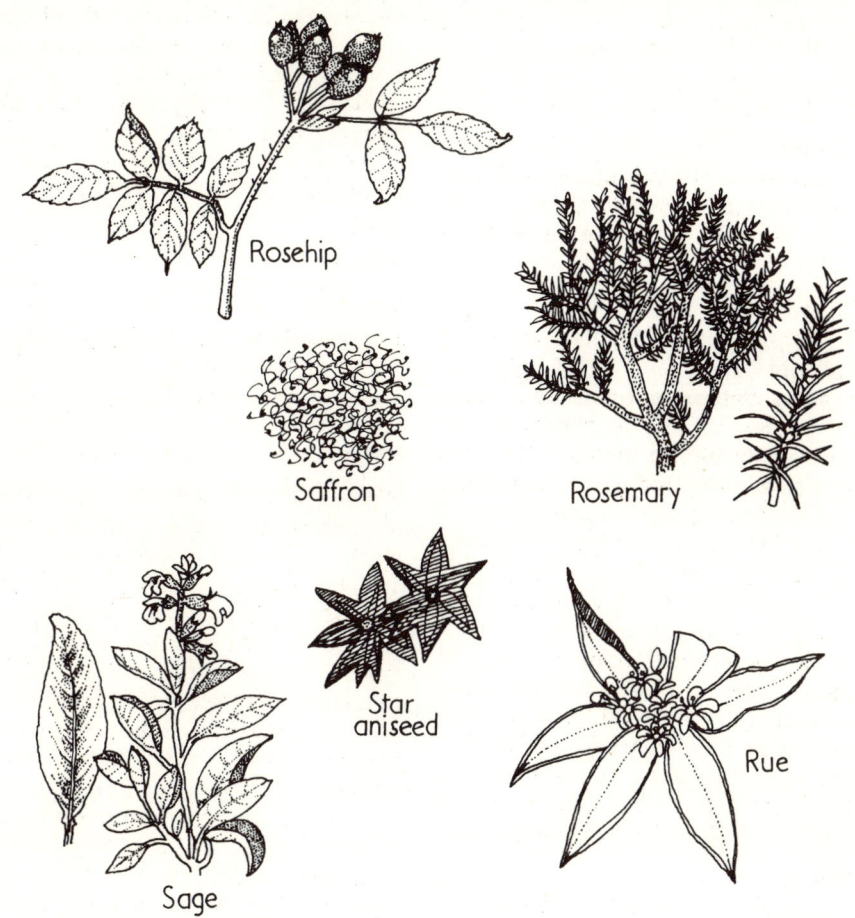

Rosehip

Saffron

Rosemary

Star aniseed

Rue

Sage

it is such a rare plant that it is almost an endangered species. American recipe books still often include recipes, and some specialist greengrocers do sell salsify root. If you have a garden or allotment, it would be an excellent crop to experiment with. Peel the roots and slice, steam, then serve with butter and pepper or with lemon juice.

Salsify has a very distinctive flavour, quite a change from other root vegetables.

Sesame
These small, teardrop-shaped beige seeds are a very good buy as they are an excellent source of protein, iron and vitamins. And with their richly savoury flavour, they go a long way – so do not be put off by the price. As well as whole sesame seeds you can buy tahini, or sesame paste, which makes an excellent sandwich spread, sauce, salad dressing or even custard. A few ideas with sesame seeds are given below.

An alphabet of herbs and spices

Gomasio

Combine 5 parts sesame seeds, toasted, with 1 part sea salt. Grind, or put in a salt mill, and use as a table condiment.

Sesame fruit balls

Soak equal parts of dates and dried apricots overnight, drain off the soaking water and reduce to a purée by grinding in a pestle and mortar or passing through a blender, then roll into small balls; roll these generously in a coating of sesame seeds.

In addition you can include sesame seeds in granola mixtures, put them into the topping for savoury or sweet crumbles and use as a topping for loaves and bread rolls, secured in place with a glaze of egg yolk. Vegetables such as cabbage or carrot are more interesting for children if you sprinkle over a few toasted seeds just before serving. Good in salads and in Chinese fried vegetables also.

Sorrel

There are two varieties of sorrel – wild and cultivated. The cultivated variety is almost never seen in the shops, but it is very easy to grow. It looks exactly like spinach but tastes like lemons. Wild sorrel is a very common wild plant with spiky flowers which change from green to red. More rangy than the cultivated plant, the leaves are large and narrow. As soon as you nibble one you will be sure of your identification, for these too taste of lemon.

A few raw sorrel leaves make a tasty addition to mixed salads. They appear very early in spring so are useful when greens are expensive in the shops. Do not eat too much too often, however, because like all spinach-family plants they contain oxalic acid and you can have too much of that. It slows down the rate at which your red blood cells absorb nutrients. Steam, or make sorrel soup.

Sorrel soup

4oz sorrel
1 large potato
1 tbsp cooking oil
1 tbsp whole wheat flour
1pt milk
salt and white pepper to taste

Wash and finely chop the sorrel. Peel the potato and boil it till tender, then mash. Put the oil in a soup saucepan and heat gently. Add the flour to form a roux and when the flour has cooked in the oil for a few minutes, start to trickle in the milk slowly so that the flour thickens smoothly. As you go, add the salt and white pepper. Now very carefully and gradually stir in first the mashed potato and then the sorrel. Continue to simmer gently until the sorrel becomes really tender, almost dissolving into the white sauce. Serve with toast.

Star aniseed

This has a slightly more subtle taste than ordinary aniseed. The only place I have always found it is in Chinese supermarkets. It really is an intriguing spice – the seed-pod must be a dried flower, for it is brown like wood, usually about an inch across and shaped like a star or flower, but with a shiny brown seed inside each 'petal'. Put one 'flower' into any stew or casserole and discard at the end of cooking.

34

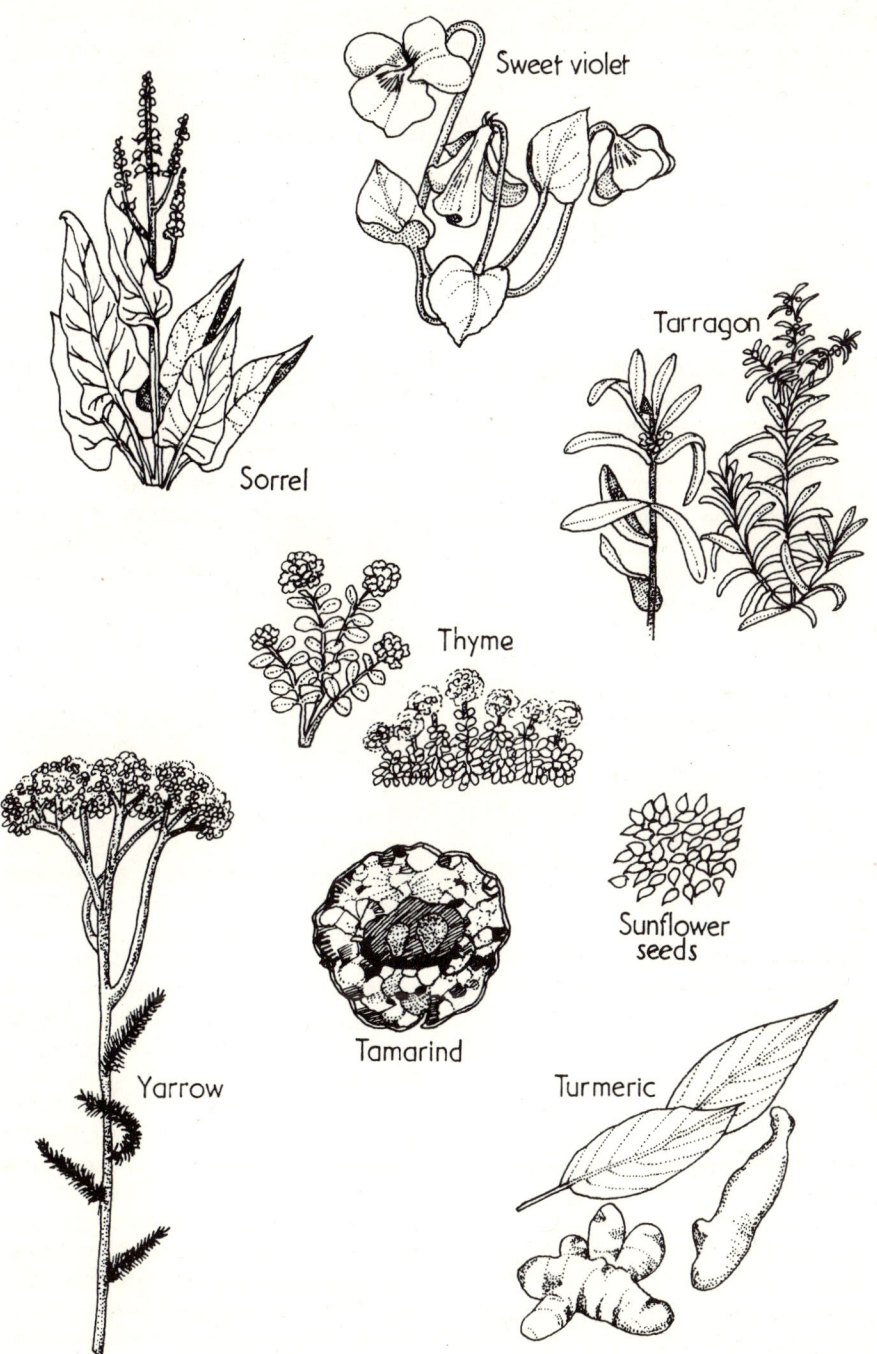

Sweet violet

Sorrel

Tarragon

Thyme

Yarrow

Tamarind

Sunflower seeds

Turmeric

35

An alphabet of herbs and spices

Sunflower seed

An excellent source of protein which, in many traditional cultures, is considered an aid to virility. I bake it into both sweet and savoury crumbles, into breads and into granola. The seeds are greyish, about the size of a sweetcorn kernel, and they have a flavour something like peanut butter but sweeter and subtler.

You can also buy an excellent sunflower butter in health-food shops and this has been popular with everyone I know who has tried it.

Tamarind

A citrus fruit, which is not edible raw but which is dried and pressed into blocks rather resembling dates. A small lump is broken off and steeped in hot water to form a citrus-flavoured sauce much used in South Indian cookery. You could always substitute lemon juice in a recipe, but if you want to experiment with tamarind it is available from well-stocked Asian grocers and has the advantage that it will keep in the fridge and can be used when you do not have a lemon.

Tarragon

You could try growing your own tarragon in the garden; it is a large, bushy perennial. But if you want to experiment, use small amounts of the dried herb. Use it in an interesting herbal butter to garnish individual side vegetables, it is also very well suited to salad dressings and sauces.

To make your own tarragon vinegar or tarragon French dressing, submerge a large sprig of the herb in the bottle and leave to stand, then continue using little by little.

Thyme

One of the commonest of culinary herbs, this is a small plant with purple flowers which is easy to grow in a pot or window-box. Fresh thyme is excellent in very small amounts in mixed salad, especially if this contains tomatoes. Useful for herb butters, French dressing, for any dish containing tomatoes and for casseroles and stews. Also a suitable ingredient for 'mixed herbs'. You can include thyme in mixed-herb teas if used sparingly. Wild thyme is more delicate in both flavour and perfume. One of my most exquisite memories is walking barefoot on a hot summer's day across the wild thyme lawn at Polesden Lacey, a National Trust property in Surrey. Heady days!

Turmeric

An essential ingredient in all curry powders, useful in colouring rice for party dishes, and good play food: Indian peasant women paint their hands and faces with turmeric for weddings and your children might like to; it is very harmless mild stuff. They can also practise tie-dying with turmeric, though sadly the resulting patterns will not be colour-fast. Turmeric is actually a dried and ground root related to ginger, but it is strong only in colour. The flavour and aroma are quite bland. The main problem is that turmeric is often stale. But if you like making curries, it is an essential ingredient. Use it quite liberally.

Verbena, lemon

One of the best known of herb teas, and deservedly so. When steeped the dried leaves release a wonderful lemon fragrance. The pale green tea is very light in flavour. One of the most highly regarded of the French tisanes, it is a relaxing tea, useful for inducing sleep and relieving tension.

Violet, sweet

Candied violets are quite famous but I do not make them because of the sugar involved.

But for a flavour of the past, use violet petals in your favourite milk puddings.

Yarrow

A very easy herb to gather from the wild. It blooms in late summer and its fronds of dark-green feathery leaves, the tall stems, and the umbrels of white or pinkish flowers are unmistakable. Robust specimens are especially common near water. Both flower heads and leaves can be gathered and dried to make a herb tea, which I like immensely, for its aroma is savoury rather than sweet. It is a golden-green and very light in flavour. I have tried it fresh in salads, where the aroma and flavour were delightful but I found the texture a bit too furry for my liking.

Buying and storing herbs and spices

In a health-food cook's kitchen, the herb and spice rack should have pride of place: no longer should there be a dark neglected corner of the cupboard where, dusty, stale and forlorn, sit the pepper, mustard and cinnamon, and not much else. Herbs and spices should be included daily and liberally in your cooking. Economical buying is going to be very important if you want to use these foods in large quantities: realistically, many readers will not have the time, space or inclination to grow their own. Useful sources of supply to hunt out in your area are: herbalists, herbalist chemists, health food and wholefood shops, and Asian grocers, especially the larger Asian supermarkets, both Indo-Pakistani and Chinese.

Remember to buy herbs in small quantities, no more than two ounces at a time, unless you know you will use them more quickly, but buy them loose to avoid expensive packaging. Buy your spices whole rather than powdered whenever possible, then you can buy and store larger quantities safely. Garlic, ginger and chilli can all be bought fresh but examine them carefully to make sure they are in perfect condition. The price can vary enormously. Recently I found root ginger in Birmingham for 40p per pound while in the same week it was 90p per pound where I live. The cheap ginger was in excellent condition!

When storing herbs at home, keep them in jars which have been sterilized and thoroughly dried so that no mould can form, and label the jars clearly — even an experienced cook can be mystified to find a jar of nondescript grey-green stuff or brown powder in the odd corner! Keep the jars away from direct sunlight and not in an overheated place, and all should be well.

If you do want to grind your own spices freshly, then buy sturdy utensils. You might break the blades of a flimsy blender on your peppercorns. Spice mills and pestle and mortar especially must be really workmanlike, not purely decorative in cheap wood which cracks after a few vigorous sessions of crunching and pounding.

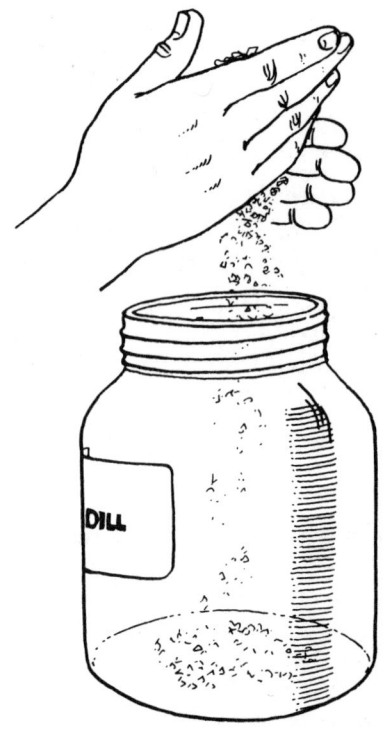

Combining herbs and spices

As far as I am concerned there are only two basic rules: do not use stale herbs, and do not bother with commercially ready-mixed herb blends. I find it quite irritating to be told that a particular herb can only be used with fish or can never be used with cabbage. How limiting for the inexperienced cook who feels obliged to present herbs in some socially acceptable setting.

What you need to do is to taste each individual herb properly and decide what you like to do with it, and what the people you are cooking for like. Then go ahead and do exactly what you like with confidence. You will make the occasional error: I once went mad with a large sprig of fresh sage and cooked a stew I still cannot forget. I wish I could . . . But I am not going to be told that I cannot eat mint sauce because I am a vegetarian – of course there are vegetarian dishes which suit mint sauce, and with a bit of thought I have found some of them.

Salad herbs
To take advantage of these you must either grow a few herbs somewhere or be prepared to gather them from the wild. Even if you live in the heart of a big city there must be waste ground, canal banks or country walks nearby where you can gather a few herbs.

But a warning: avoid roadside verges where you can be sure the poor plants are poisonous with their rich coating of lead and car fumes.

Spices to use in salads include aniseed, caraway seed, fresh chilli, coriander seed, cummin seed, garlic, grated root ginger, pepper.

When first experimenting, put just a small amount of one or two herbs into a mixed salad and see how you like them. They fall into two groups, the strong-flavoured ones and the blander vegetable-style herbs which can be used more liberally.

Strong herbs
Chamomile (fresh only), dandelion leaf, elder shoots, fennel (seeds or stem), juniper berries, marshmallow, mint (all varieties), nasturtium leaves, oregano, rosemary, rue, sage, sorrel, thyme, yarrow.

Bland herbs
Alfalfa, angelica stems, borage, celeriac, wild chervil, chickweed, chicory, chives, sweet cicely, comfrey (very young leaves), coriander greens, lemon balm, marigold flower, marjoram, nasturtium flower, nasturtium seed (fresh), parsley, rose petal, sesame seed, sunflower seed.

Salad dressings
Basic French dressing (oil and vinegar) can be a different experience every time you make it. If you prepare a jar and steep some fresh herb in it, then keep it in the fridge or a cool place, gradually it will become more and more herbal. Suitable herbs are basil, oregano, tarragon, thyme, rosemary and sage. But you can also make French dressing pungent by beating in a little crushed garlic or mustard powder. Make it with fruit juice instead of vinegar sometimes: lemon, orange and grapefuit all work well, or tamarind steeped in hot water.

Combining herbs and spices

I often use a little of either coriander or cummin seed crushed into French dressing. The cummin is especially good with cucumber and tomato, while coriander is superb with most salads but especially with aubergine or avocado. And if I make a lentil salad I sometimes use a little chopped fresh green chilli in the dressing. Mountains of cold beans can be very bland and the occasional tingle of fresh chilli livens them up tremendously. Grated or crushed ginger is just as lively, and sweeter.

An extremely easy, nourishing and tasty form of salad dressing is yoghurt, beaten and salted and thinned if necessary, and poured over the salad at the last moment (so that the greens do not wilt). Any fresh savoury herb of your choice added will make an interesting dressing, but particularly striking are: raw onion, chives, garlic, mint, coriander, cummin, chilli, dill or caraway (individually, of course, not in combination!).

Herbal fruit salads
Try any of these ingredients in fruit salads for a new flavour and texture: the petals of marigolds, nasturtiums, violets or roses, sesame or sunflower seeds, alfalfa or other beansprouts raw, angelica stems (raw), lightly crushed aniseed, lightly crushed caraway seed, sweet cicely, cinnamon, elderflower, fennel seeds or stems, a tiny touch of grated ginger root, juniper berries, lemon balm, lemon geranium, all varieties of mint, nutmeg.

Flavouring cooked fruit
Stewed fruit, fruit crumbles, fruit pies and baked fruit can be greatly enhanced by a light use of herbs and spices. For example, whenever you can get fresh angelica or sweet cicely stems and cook these with the fruit, you need much less sugar. A little finely crushed mint cooked in with summer fruits which are then served cold can give them a lift.

Be sparing with spices, but be flexible. Apples, for example, can be cooked in a pie or crumble, or stewed with either cardamom or clove, but in the oven you might try them with either cinnamon or caraway seed. On some occasions, ginger is good with apple.

I find that a little fennel or aniseed (used very lightly) will lighten the flavour of a tart batch of fruit. In pies I especially like to add a few juniper berries. When fruit is served cold, decorate with flower petals and grated coconut or nuts.

Herbs and spices in teas
Almost all the leafy herbs and all the dried-flower herbs can be used in herb teas. These can be drunk plain or with honey, or honey and lemon if you prefer, and they can be drunk hot or chilled. You should experiment with the individual herb as a tea and then build up blends to suit your own taste.

Try any of these alone or in combination: chamomile, comfrey, elderflower, eucalyptus, heather flower, hibiscus, horsetail, jasmine, juniper, lavender, lady's mantle, lemon balm, lime blossom, marigold, marshmallow root, mint (all forms), nettle, raspberry leaf, rose petals, dried and crushed rose-hip, rosemary, rue, sage, thyme, lemon verbena, yarrow.

Seeds and spices suitable for teas include: aniseed, cardamom, cinnamon, clove, coriander seed, fennel seed, ginger, ginseng, nutmeg, black pepper, star aniseed. (These should be used in mixtures and blended with a good quality of black tea, one teaspoon of mixed spices per pot of tea. This kind of spiced tea, called *masala chai* is a winter tonic drink in North India, toning up the respiratory system and effectively reducing the severity of colds and flu if taken regularly.)

Savoury herbal mixtures

White sauce
Bay, fennel, garlic, a touch of ginger, horseradish, lemon geranium, marigold (for colour), nutmeg, parsley, white pepper, poppy seed (crushed), saffron, sorrel, turmeric (for colour), violet (for puddings).

Tomato sauce
Basil, bay, cayenne, chervil, chilli, cummin, garlic, ginger, juniper, mint, oregano, paprika, black pepper, sweet peppers, tamarind, thyme.

Brown sauce and gravy
(especially those made with miso and tamari or yeast)
Aniseed, chervil, chilli, coriander, fennel, garlic, ginger, marjoram, oregano, black pepper, sweet pepper, rosemary, sorrel, star aniseed, tamarind, thyme.

Soups and stews
Aniseed, arrowroot, basil, bay, borage, chervil, chilli, comfrey, coriander, cummin, dandelion leaf or root, fennel seed, garam masala (in stews), garlic, ginger, juniper, lovage, marjoram, mint (summer soups), nettle (fresh), oregano, paprika, parsley (fresh), black pepper, sweet pepper, poppy seed, sorrel, star aniseed (stews), tamarind (for a sweet and sour taste), thyme.

Rissoles and nut roasts
A little sage and rosemary in combination with some thyme or marjoram or oregano or basil as you wish and a touch of pepper is a good herbal blend. Chopped onion should be one of the ingredients.

For more pungent mixtures use garlic and paprika and a touch of coriander or ginger or chilli and season with tamari rather than salt.

Omelettes, quiches and other egg dishes
Garlic or chives or spring onions are better than ordinary onions. Black and white pepper each have their own special effect. A tiny suggestion of chilli or paprika can be a pleasant surprise. A touch of mustard is good if your egg is combined with cheese; so too is caraway seed. A sprinkling of nutmeg on top of a quiche enhances the flavour. My favourite herbs are marjoram, oregano and thyme.

Oven-baked savoury pies and crumbles
These are big dishes and they can be more bland and stodgy than you bargained for, so you should not be timid in seasoning. Garlic, black pepper, ginger and paprika are all useful strong flavours. Garam masala, coriander seed, sesame seed, sunflower seed, caraway seed and nutmeg all give a lively savoury taste to oven-baked dishes. My favourite herbs for oven baking are sage, rosemary and oregano.

Combining herbs and spices

Casseroles

Aniseed, basil, bay, cayenne, chervil, chilli, clove, comfrey, coriander, cummin, curry leaf, fennel, garam masala, garlic, ginger, juniper, lovage, marjoram, mustard, nutmeg, oregano, paprika, black pepper, sweet pepper, poppy seed, rosemary, sage, star aniseed, thyme.

Individual vegetables

We all know that peas, especially elderly peas, can be made more palatable by the addition to the cooking water of some fresh mint. Variations on this theme are endless and can turn a common vegetable into an elegant dish, or tempt children to eat an unpopular old standard like carrots or cabbage. Below are a few ideas which I find work well, but I hope you will experiment to suit your own tastes.

Potatoes can be mashed with raw onion, chives, parsley, or coriander greens. Boiled potatoes can be served with fennel or parsley sauce or with a herb butter or with caraway-seed butter. When baked, roasted or sautéed, potatoes can be dusted with coriander or garam masala at the end of cooking. A baked potato can be smothered in yoghurt flavoured with salt and mint. Potato curry is the equivalent of fish and chips in Indian cafés.

Carrots can be steamed and served with a touch of cummin, with toasted sesame seeds or with herb butter.

Serve **cabbage** with toasted nuts, or put a few dill seeds or cloves into the cooking water (discard them before eating).

Sweet vegetables, such as pumpkin, carrot, parsnip, swede and turnip suit coriander, garam masala, ginger and nutmeg.

Tomatoes, either raw or cooked, are delectable with cummin, with coriander greens or with thyme.

Try **broccoli** or **cauliflower** with nutmeg, caraway or fennel. Generally speaking, liven up the vegetables you tend to take for granted, but let the more unusual vegetables speak for themselves. For all vegetables, if bought, cooked and eaten in good condition, have distinctive and delicious flavours of their own which we should learn to appreciate.

Cakes and biscuits

Generally speaking, use the spices in their dried and ground form and sieve them into the flour very thoroughly so that their flavour is evenly distributed throughout the cake. The exception to this rule is seeds. Caraway, poppy seed, sesame seed and sunflower seed are all useful in cakes and biscuits. If they are to be buried deep inside the dough, then toast them lightly first to enhance their flavour. But if they are to garnish the top of a cake or biscuit, do not cook them first and add them as late in the baking as possible so that they do not scorch. Whole or chopped nuts should be treated in the same way.

Another book in this series, *Health Food Baking,* gives plenty of individual recipes, but here are some useful hints.

Cinnamon, nutmeg and dried ginger are all excellent in cakes and biscuits, as are the seeds mentioned above. When making very heavily spiced cakes or heavy fruit cakes you can also put in some coriander, cardamom or garam masala, or allspice.

Spice mixture

For a heavy fruit cake use equal amounts of cinnamon, nutmeg and coriander with half as much of ginger and a half teaspoon of crushed cardamom. Or combine garam masala and ginger, a touch of clove and a pinch of mace. For a lighter spicy cake use one measure of ginger to half a measure each of nutmeg and cinnamon. When cooking with honey or treacle, ginger and caraway are the best spices to use.

Loaves and rolls

If you have a good basic whole wheat bread recipe you can try several tasty additions, so that each loaf is different. If you glaze the tops of loaves or rolls with egg yolk you can sprinkle on raw poppy, sesame or sunflower seeds, bran or chopped nuts, and then bake as normally. If you toast sesame or sunflower seeds you can mix them into the bread dough. Crushed garlic can similarly be worked into the dough.

If you have some leftover grain or vegetable, you can mash this thoroughly and add 1 tsp of the herbs of your choice, and then work the mixture into your bread dough in the early, moist stages of the bread making. Allow no more than two tablespoons (heaped) of mush for each one pound loaf you are making. This makes an excellent savoury bread which is naturally a little heavier in texture than a pure grain bread.

For a sweet loaf, add 1 dessertspoon black strap molasses, one flat dessertspoon currants and a generous pinch of powdered cinnamon to your dough for each one pound loaf.

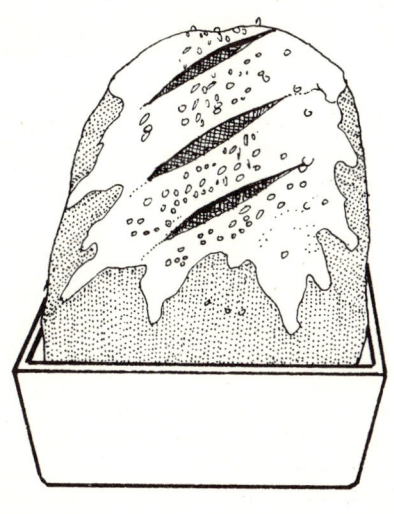

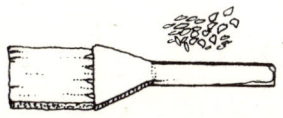

Combining herbs and spices

Pickles and chutneys

Do not eat too many pickles and chutneys — they are obviously not as nutritious as fresh fruit and vegetables and were a compromise in days when fresh food was almost unobtainable in winter. Now we can have fresh food all year round. Commercial preserves are generally made using white sugar, chemical preservatives and colourings and the cheaper and harsher forms of vinegar. Home-made pickles and chutneys will contain no chemicals and you can use a good wine or cider vinegar and pure brown sugar.

European-style

If you wish to pickle onions, beetroot, cabbage, gherkins or mixed vegetables, then basically you should use salt, vinegar and not very much else. You do not want a muddle of heavy flavours or the quality of the original vegetable will be lost. Suitable spices are black peppercorns, allspice, mace, dill, cloves, ginger and mustard seed. Select only one or two from this list, according to your own taste and their availability.

Indian style

I have been collecting pickle recipes from Indian friends and from recipe books over the years, and I like the true achars, or marinated pickles, very much. The fruits and vegetables are preserved by storing for a long period in either salt alone (as in some recipes for lemon or lime pickle) or in

salt and oil which has been heated. (Mustard oil is most often recommended.) At first the fruit or vegetable has to be kept in a warm place and shaken daily, but after about a week it can be stored like any other preserve for as long as possible so that the flavours mature. To this basic recipe quite pungent spices can be added, such as garlic, chilli, ginger and mustard seed, but any of the lighter aromatic spices can be added to suit your taste.

Here are two recipes I personally like very much.

Lemon achar

10 small lemons in excellent condition
1pt of a good vegetable oil (preferably mustard oil)
1 heaped tbsp salt
4 dried red chilli pods, bruised but left whole
1 medium ginger root, peeled and chopped
1 heaped tbsp of a mixture of the following whole spices: black peppercorns, cummin seeds and mustard seeds

Prepare a bottle large enough to hold all the ingredients by sterilizing it thoroughly and keeping it warm. Quarter the lemons leaving the skins intact and remove the seeds, then arrange them in the jar. Put the oil, salt, whole spices, chilli and ginger in a saucepan, heat it carefully till it is very hot, then lower the heat and simmer for 5 more minutes, then pour over the lemons and seal.

For the first week keep in a warm place and shake gently once a day, then store with your other preserves and allow to mature. You could use limes instead.

Mixed vegetable achar

1½lb mixture of the following raw vegetables: onions, peeled and sliced, cauliflower broken in small flowerettes, carrot peeled and sliced in strips, cucumber (unpeeled) sliced in rounds
1 heaped tbsp salt
4 small green chillis
1 heaped tbsp of mixed aniseed, coriander seed and cummin seed
1pt good vegetable oil, preferably mustard oil

Sterilize and warm a large preserving jar. Clean and trim all the vegetables and arrange them in the jar, sprinkling with salt as you go. Put the chilli and other spices into the oil in a saucepan and heat as high as possible, then lower the flame and simmer for 5 minutes before pouring over the vegetables. Seal and keep in a warm place for a week, shaking daily. Leave for as long as possible to mature before eating.

Chutney

Basically you will be cooking the fruits or vegetables of your choice in wine or cider vinegar with brown sugar and spices, then bottling them like jam.

Mild and sweet

For a 4lb batch of chutney (ie, when you are using 2lb of fruit, slightly less than 2lb of sugar and a half pint of vinegar) you should include 1 small clove of garlic, 1oz of root ginger, a generous pinch of chilli and then make your own selection from these spice seeds: coriander, fennel, cummin, mustard, caraway, black peppercorns and cardamom or clove, and mace.

Hot

For the same amount of chutney, increase the ginger to two ounces, use 4 green or red dried chilli pods, finely chopped, and be sure to include black peppercorns and mustard seed among your choice from the list of spice seeds.

In selecting the spices be guided by the spices you like with the particular fruits or vegetables you are preserving in other dishes, eg if you particularly like cloves with apples be sure to include clove in apple chutney.

Curries

A book on herbs and spices should not neglect curries. I have always considered Indian cuisine to be the finest of vegetarian cuisines and have learned a lot from Indian friends. We are sure to eat curry at least once a week at home and I try to prepare curries very much as an Indian vegetarian housewife would. Ready-made curry mixtures are all-purpose affairs, and are naturally more suited to heavy meat dishes than to vegetables, so I do not buy them. In any case they may not be fresh, and every curry made with them will taste pretty much the same. If you buy all your spices fresh and grind or chop them immediately before use, you will be surprised to find that they are not the pungent, oily, strong-smelling affairs of Indian restaurants. The restaurants in this country, with a few honourable exceptions, have adapted to English taste and expectations just as completely as the corner Chinese take-away has, and although I enjoy the food served in Indian restaurants I know it is quite different from the food eaten in Indian homes. The recipes below come closer.

Combining herbs and spices

General technique

Whatever curry you are making, the ginger, garlic and chilli will be in the whole fresh form and should be peeled, chopped and crushed first. The other spices will be either whole or in dry powder form. These should all be crushed and blended as finely as possible.

Now the oil for cooking, the onion for seasoning and the vegetable ingredients should be prepared, and in the vast majority of curry recipes you will begin by heating the oil, lightly frying the onion and the crushed wet spices, adding the dried mixed spices and frying for a minute or two longer, then adding the vegetables or pulses and coating well in the spicy oil. Finally water is added and the dish is allowed to simmer gently until the vegetables are tender.

If you want a 'dry' curry, use just enough liquid to cover, and if it seems too moist cook uncovered. For a 'wet' curry, cover the ingredients generously with liquid and cook covered. Apart from water, other liquids which blend well with curry spices are milk or yoghurt (korma curry), tamarind steeped in hot water (for a sweet and sour curry), whey, coconut milk and tomato paste.

In general, use the very hot spices such as chilli, ginger and pepper as a basic measure and use at least double that amount of the lighter spices such as turmeric, coriander, cummin or fennel. For a pot of curry sufficient for 4 to 6 people, a generous tea-spoon of the hot spices would be a basic measure and the rest in proportion (or 2 small fresh chilli pods); for a milder curry use half a teaspoon of the hot spices as the basic measure, with the rest in proportion. That suits me as I do not like hot curry, preferring to be able to taste the other flavours. So *you* might like to increase my proportions. However, for anyone timid and unsure I am certain the basic half-teaspoon would be a safe measure for first experiments.

Hot curry (suitable for a large pot of mixed vegetables)

1 large or 2 small green chilli pods, finely minced
1 small clove of garlic, peeled and crushed
1 flat tsp freshly ground black pepper
2 heaped tsp turmeric
2 generous tsp each of coriander, cummin and mustard seed
1 bay leaf
1½ in piece of root ginger

Mild curry (for a large pot of vegetables)

1 tsp paprika
½ tsp freshly crushed black pepper
1in piece of root ginger
4 cloves of garlic, peeled and crushed
1 heaped tsp turmeric
1 heaped tsp each of coriander, fennel *or* aniseed *or* caraway, cardamom *or* clove, and cinnamon

Lentil curry

1 clove garlic, peeled and crushed
1 heaped tsp paprika
1 flat tsp freshly ground black pepper
1in piece root ginger, crushed
1 heaped tsp turmeric
1 heaped tsp each of cummin, mustard and caraway

Lemon and butter should be added at the end and if possible coriander greens used as a garnish.

Spiced side vegetables

These are cooked with a very light hand indeed. Generally speaking, turmeric is included to give a pleasant golden colour but only one or two spices to enhance the particular vegetable will be used. Here are some of my favourites.

Potato, caraway and coriander, or garam masala, with pepper;
Carrot, ginger and cummin;
Cauliflower, cummin and caraway with white pepper;
Sweet potato, as for potato;
Bindi, (also called okra or lady's finger), ginger, lemon juice, coriander;
Aubergine, coriander, black pepper and ginger;
Swede or turnip, coriander and nutmeg or cinnamon with pepper;
Green beans, coconut, coriander and mustard seed with pepper;
Green peas, (cook in butter), garlic, pepper and coriander;
Cabbage, coconut, cummin, garlic and pepper;
Tomato, black pepper, cummin, bay, garlic and paprika;
Mushroom, caraway, black pepper and coriander.

Do not thicken curry sauces with flour or cornflour as this kills the flavour of the spices. Traditionally milk or yoghurt thicken the sauce, which is formed only from the vegetable juices and can be thickened by evaporation. Do not include fresh or dried fruits if you want an authentic curry — these are purely Anglo-Indian in origin. European root vegetables and Brussels sprouts do not blend well in curry dishes; they are rarely seen in India and do not suit the traditional recipes.

If a curry is too bland, you can add a little more chilli but you must leave it to stand and then reheat or you will taste raw chilli in the dish. If it is too hot add sugar, milk or yoghurt to the sauce as you think appropriate, blend well, then reheat. Eat yoghurt and sweet mild chutneys to cool the palate rather than drinking water with curries.

Conversion Tables

Oven temperatures

Gas Mark			
½	250°F	120°C
1	275°F	140°C
2	300°F	150°C
3	325°F	170°C
4	350°F	180°C
5	375°F	190°C
6	400°F	200°C
7	425°F	220°C
8	450°F	230°C
9	475°F	240°C

Liquid measures (approximate conversions)

1pt (20fl oz)	570ml
½pt (10fl oz)	275
¼pt (5fl oz)	150

Liquid measures (approximate conversions)

1 mug (8fl oz)	250
1 cup (6fl oz)	168
1 level tablespoon (1fl oz)	25
1 level dessertspoon (½fl oz)	12
1 level teaspoon (1/6fl oz)	5

Dry weights (approximate conversions)

1lb (16oz)	450g
½lb (8oz)	225
¼lb (4oz)	110
1oz	25
1 mug (8oz)	225
1 cup flour (5oz)	125
1 cup rice (6oz)	175
1 tablespoon (1oz)	25
1 dessertspoon (⅔oz)	18
1 teaspoon (⅓oz)	9

Thanks are due to Cranks Health Foods, and particularly to the Manager of Cranks Restaurant, Dartington, Devon for his kind assistance with the front cover photograph.

British Library Cataloguing in Publication Data
Young, Mala
  Health food cooking, herbs and spices.
  1. Vegetarian cookery
  2. Spices
  3. Cookery (Herbs)
  I. Title
  641.6' 3' 83   TX837

  ISBN 0−7153−8040−0

Library of Congress Catalog Card Number: 80−68703

Text and illustrations © David & Charles Ltd, 1981
Illustrated by Susan Neale

Typeset in 10 on 11 point Univers by Typesetters (Birmingham) Ltd. and printed in Great Britain
by Redwood Burn Limited, Trowbridge & Esher
for David & Charles (Publishers) Limited
Brunel House   Newton Abbot   Devon